From a Poor Boy
to
a Successful Man

Jim Gardner

ISBN 978-1-62806-379-0 (print | paperback)
ISBN 978-1-62806-381-3 (ebook)

Library of Congress Control Number 2023909528

Published by Salt Water Media
29 Broad Street, Suite 104
Berlin, MD 21811
www.saltwatermedia.com

Salt Water
MEDIA

Cover image by the author
Interior images by the author

From a Poor Boy
to
a Successful Man

Dedication

I dedicate this book to all my family members, both those living and those to come. May it help them understand our ancestors and their lives.

Contents

My Faith

I was raised a Catholic. My grandmother was the one who brought the Catholic religion into the family; my grandfather, whom she married, was not Catholic. We had this habit of going to church on Sundays and other required days. There were very few Catholics in my community of Greensboro, Maryland. So Catholics were seldom included in social gatherings.

During the years I spent in the Navy, I maintained my faith even though I often got off track, but I was soon back on the path I had hopped off from. When I left the Navy and married, my wife became a Catholic, and we were married in the church, but my siblings left the Catholic faith and followed some other belief systems.

My four children were raised Catholic. Two of my daughters are practicing Catholics, and their children are all practicing Catholics as well. At age eighty-four, I continue to practice my religion, but unfortunately, my partner left a bit early.

My Wife

Rosalie and I started dating in 1958 while I was in the Navy, but we saw each other only when I could get leave for a few days. I would drive home from Charleston, South Carolina, when the submarine I was stationed on came into port for a few days. I would get home late Friday night or early Saturday morning and leave Sunday afternoon. We usually went to a movie or just spent time together at my house or hers. I would have to drive nearly all night and get back around 3 a.m. I often did not have enough money for gasoline, so I would drive through Washington D.C. looking for sailors standing close to the road. I would stop and ask if they needed a ride. If they did and had a couple of dollars to help with gasoline, I would tell them to get in. If they had no money, I would continue on until I found someone with a couple of dollars.

We were married on December 17, 1960, about three weeks after I was discharged from the Navy. Rosie had a beautiful wedding gown. I think she only had about two months to prepare for the wedding. We were married at Immaculate Conception Catholic Church in Marydel, Maryland, and we held the reception at the Marydel firehouse. It had snowed all week, and the roads were nearly closed. Hugh snow drifts were all along the roads and the roads had several inches of snow on them. The only money we had for a honeymoon was money we received at the reception. The people who attended the wedding donated the food. Each family brought a large supply of their favorite dish. Rosie's father furnished the homemade wine.

Rosie would have liked to have attended college, but her father told her it was a waste to spend money on sending a girl to college as her place was in the home.

Her brother Carl graduated from college and became vice-president of ILC Dover and earned a very high salary. We had always been close to Carl and his wife. Rosie was a beautiful young girl and maintained her beauty throughout her entire life.

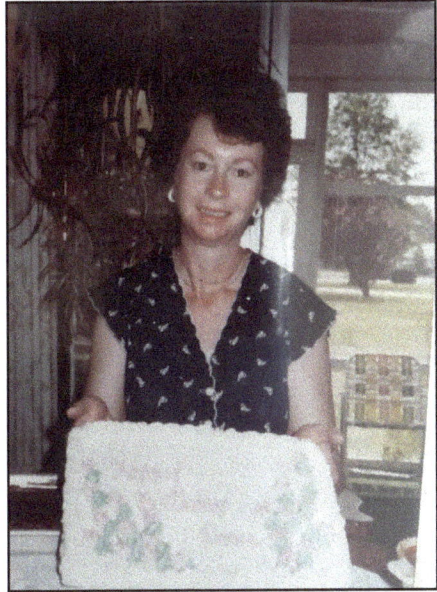

Rosie

Even at 72 years old and near death, she still had beautiful skin with no wrinkles.

We had a good marriage, going to church nearly every Sunday. She made sure the girls were well dressed for church. She would always make a fine Sunday dinner with plenty to eat for all. When her mother, Marie, was diagnosed with breast cancer, Rosie always took her to Wilmington, Delaware, for treatment. That trip was about a hundred miles each way.

I know one time her mother did not have money to pay off the weekly charge bill at a grocery store. Rosie gave her the money, but her mother asked her never to tell her father, as he would be mad that she did not have the money. Her mother would save a few cents from the groceries each week so that she would have money for Christmas. Rosie and her mother would make special cakes to sell at Christmas time. Rosie would give samples to people on the street and ask them if they wanted to order one for Christmas.

After her mother died, Rosie would have her father over for dinner on Wednesday night and he would stay the night; she would always send him home with enough for several days. Her father never cooked, but after a while, he learned how to at least make a cup of tea.

Rosie also cared for one of our neighbors in Seaford, taking her to Wilmington for cancer treatments and would not accept money for gas or other expenses. She was always available to help others.

She really enjoyed working with the Girl Scouts for several years, and worked at the state park in Laurel, Delaware, for a few years. She never wanted extravagant things and was happy with the small things in life.

She always accepted the responsibility of keeping a clean house. She was an excellent mother and devoted whatever time required to see that the girls were well cared for.

I was always active in the Knights of Columbus, so Rosie and I went to many dinner dances over the years. We were both excellent dancers and used to attend many dances.

Rosie was diagnosed with breast cancer in 1986. She had both breasts removed and underwent a lot of chemo and radiation treatment over the next few years. After this time, she was never really healthy. She had many operations for various things and many lumps removed from her breast. She maintained a wonderful spirit during this time. She had vein troubles in her legs and had them operated on and some veins removed. In Florida, she had her left knee replaced. After the replacement, she said that a lot of the pain she had over the years had ended. She never complained much about her health and continued to maintain her religion. We were both Eucharistic Ministers in the Catholic church. Many times, when she just did not feel like going to church, I would bring Holy Communion home to her.

Rosie and I had four daughters. She had one miscarriage around 1965 and took the miscarriage very hard; I don't think she ever really got over it. I remember that after this miscarriage was the first time in our marriage that Rosie ever displayed anger toward me. She was kind and loving towards me most of the time, but the miscarriage took a toll on her. She lost the fetus at home with no medical support. She suffered for several days, and the family doctor just said that if we lost the baby, it was God's will.

She loved both country music and classical music. Her favorite entertainer of all time was Elvis. I always bought her his records and tapes and finally CDs.

Rosie never asked for much and was happy to just go out and eat occasionally. We visited New York City to see a play occasionally. We enjoyed going to Radio City Music Hall. Being from the country, it was a joy to just walk the streets in Times Square area and see people different from us.

It was a genuine pleasure raising four girls, and I tried hard to be a good father while also earning enough money to support the large family as well as I could. At one time, I was working for DuPont as a machinist, and doing carpenter work on the side. I used to go to college at nighttime to earn my real estate license.

I decided that if I could not earn a million dollars by age 40, then I would spend what I had made up until that point and enjoy life. I never earned the million dollars, so I was not obsessed with being financially successful. I just wanted enough for my family to have some of the finer things that I did not have growing up.

We always had wonderful birthday parties for all the girls and made every effort to have them join and participate in various clubs. None of the girls had much interest in sports. Dorothy was somewhat of a tomboy and liked to do outside things and ride a motorcycle. I used to take the girls with me to the county dump to deliver our trash to the landfill. We would stop at the little store by the dump and get a Popsicle for a treat.

The girls would often help me make wine in the garage at our home on Stein Highway. They would step on the grapes with their bare feet and mash them up. I remember Dorothy tried to chew tobacco when she was around 12 years old. Her reaction was priceless.

Our Children

Karen was born in 1962. I remember I got a 1954 Mustang when she was 16 and she really loved the car and drove it to school every day. It also ran really well. I did all my own tune-up requirements. When she got home from school one day, I noticed the engine did not sound too good as it had a significant miss. Karen said that she did not know any reason why it was missing. I determined that one of the cylinders on the V-8 was not firing. The problem was inside the engine. I pulled the head and found a burnt valve. After buying a new valve, I put the valve assembly back together and reinstalled the head. The engine again ran like a new one. Many years later, I found out that Karen had been racing another student before school that day. It seems that she won the race.

Karen worked at several jobs continuously since she was 17 years old. First, she worked in a grocery store and then in a credit card cost center for banking. She then accepted a job as a manager at a distribution center that sold things wholesale to stores and to individuals through the internet. She was well paid, but the job was very demanding and stressful. She finally got into real estate maybe 15 years ago and did extremely well after earning her broker's license in both Delaware and Maryland. She managed a real estate location for Callaway, Farnell and Moore in Seaford, Delaware, for several years, but finally decided she could be more successful as an agent just listing and selling properties without the requirements of running an office. She usually earned more money than most people with a master's degree and maintained a steady clientele. She had the time and resources for three or four vacations out of the country each year and several vacations in the USA.

I remember one time in church when Karen was young and was acting up. I told her several times to behave, and she did not respond. She was probably two or three years old. I picked her up from one of the front rows in church and started towards the back. She shouted out real loud, "Daddy, don't beat me, I will behave!" The whole church got a kick out of that. She did get a little spanking downstairs and was well behaved when we went back up.

Karen had one daughter, Casey, who is the joy of her life. Casey has always been close to her mother and had been a loving daughter. She worked in a management-level position with a construction company.

Sharon was born in 1963 and had a powerful will to do things her way. She always dressed well for school. We would see that she was dressed properly when she left home. When she was 13 years old, she was physically well-developed. Men seemed to notice her early development.

Sharon became pregnant with a Black child, Marie, when she was 18. She stayed with us at home for a while but decided to find a place of her own. James was Sharon's second child and worked in several different fields. Next was Leah, who worked in the retail business. Last was Brad. He spent four years in the Navy and continued pursuing his education.

Sharon had four children with three different fathers and did not marry any of these men. She did get married for a couple of years but then separated. Sharon lived alone with her children for several years.

Marie lived with us for a few years, and we treated her as

our own daughter. She was the brightest child that I have ever known. She could talk and read when she was around two or three years old. When she was 18, I offered to send her to college. I bought her a car and got her driver's license renewed. She only went to college for a short time. She told me she wanted to be recognized as an African American and not as white. At Rosie's funeral, she hugged me and said she loved me. Sharon also attended the funeral and told me she loved me.

Sharon has a degree in nursing and has worked in that field for most of her life. We had very little loving contact with Sharon after she left home. Several of her patients in the hospital have told me she provided very loving care for them.

Dorothy was born in 1964. As a teenager, she had a B210 Datsun that she really liked. She would drive it a little fast at times. I remember one time she was stopped going to school in Georgetown, Delaware, and I think she was exceeding 70 mph. The vehicle that Dorothy really liked was the 1984 Bronco with 4-wheel drive. She used to love to take it to the beach and fish from the Atlantic shore. She worked for DuPont for a few years as an operator while attending Salisbury University. She graduated with honors while working shift work. She later left DuPont and went into a career as a social worker, mostly in the State of Delaware.

Dorothy always put her children first and went to many rock concerts, but always took the children with her, even when they were small. No matter what was going on with the two divorces, she always took excellent care of her three children. Kelley is her oldest, Mitch next, then Gabe. Kelly worked in the poultry industry after high school as a buyer of supplies, later working as a waitress in top-end restaurants. She married in her mid-20s and was devoted to her husband and her four lovely children.

She had a lot of energy and homeschooled all of her children.

As young men, both of her boys did well. Mitch graduated from Wesley College (now DSU) in Dover, Delaware, worked for Wells Fargo in a senior financial position and earned a very good salary. Gabe enlisted in the Army and adjusted well to the military. I told both that I was very proud of them. They had no problems associated with drugs or alcohol that I knew of.

Dorothy finally left Delaware after her divorce and moved to South Carolina to work in the social services field. She earned her master's degree with honors and got an excellent job in the social services field in Mecklenburg County, North Carolina. She seemed thrilled with her job. She bought a home in Pineville, North Carolina. She had never been happy living in an apartment for the few months that she had to after getting her master's degree. She was just very reluctant to try getting involved with a man at that time. She was still young enough to begin a new life with many good years in front of her. I encouraged her to keep the options open.

Lisa was born in 1971 and was the baby of the family. She stayed with us after the other girls left home. This gave her an opportunity to have a little more attention than the other girls. Lisa was always very bright. When she was in maybe the sixth grade, we decided to send her to a private school. She went to Easton, Maryland, and had some very influential students in her class, including some of the DuPont family. Lisa was always a high achiever in academics and scored in the top one and a half percent on national testing. Private schooling was very expensive and required Rosie to drive several miles each day to and from school. Lisa returned to public school for the last two or three years and did well. I think the private school was a wise investment and that it gave her a good foundation for the rest of her schooling and life.

Lisa attended Salisbury University for a couple of years and when I accepted a transfer with DuPont to Charlotte, North Carolina, she entered Western Carolina University for the rest of her education, earning a bachelor's degree. She worked in the insurance industry for most of her career and did very well. She had enough experience and did such a good job that she could change jobs at will and find new employment quickly. Lisa has maintained a close relationship with several of her college friends and they have always been there for her, and she has always been there for them. I have heard her best friend, Kirby, say that Lisa is the sister she never had. Lisa spent most of her nonworking time maintaining a good home for her husband and her son, Luke. I told Luke several times that he could not know how lucky he was to have such devoted parents. They enrolled him in every sport he was interested in, and they made sure he got the best training and support available.

Luke was normally one of the most valuable players in any of the sports that he plays. I tried to attend all his games when I was in the area. Luke attended Western Carolina University and played on a traveling baseball team for several years.

Lisa is a very devout Catholic and her husband converted to the Catholic religion. She had a real task of scheduling ball games and seeing that Luke met the requirements of attending the Catholic high school in Charlotte. Lisa and Mark and Luke were always very kind and considerate of me. I stayed at their place overnight whenever I was in the Charlotte area.

I have tried to instill some basic principles in my children and have communicated to them often that if you follow only two basic guidelines, your life will move with tranquility and will curve in the embrace of happiness.

One, always respect your neighbors and accept them as a creation of God. You don't have to accept their habits and the things you don't believe in, but you should be open enough to let them breathe in their own space. You shouldn't be intrusive and demanding. What you give, you will receive. That is how life works.

Two, always forgive anybody who causes harm to you or speaks badly of you. Don't hold grudges and burn in the fire of vengeance. Be a better man or woman and have faith in the power of good energy.

Forgiveness means not speaking ill of them unless the person you are speaking to could be harmed if you do not disclose the harm that was done to you. Never speak ill of somebody just to have a conversation. You should learn from the experience and protect yourself from the same thing happening to you again. Remain distant from the people who speak unkind words about other people. You shouldn't say or hear things about others that you can't accept for yourself.

DuPont Years

I graduated from high school in June 1956 and was offered a job at the 7UP company as a delivery truck driver. It was not a terrible job, except at the delicate age of eighteen, I was experiencing the full nightlife. I worked there for a few months and then was hired by the DuPont company for an entry-level job.

At DuPont, I started out sweeping floors all night long, working the midnight to 8 a.m. shift. It was quite boring until my supervisor provided me with an idea to feel better about my job. He advised me to be the best floor sweeper in the company and to fully clean the corners of each room. I tried this, and time seemed to go by much more easily. Next, I progressed to other low-level jobs and continued to receive better pay.

I finally took leave and joined the Navy in November 1956. The company allowed my service to continue during the four years I spent there. So, when I returned from the Navy and went back to work, I was able to get a much better blue-collar job.

I finally could bid on a maintenance job that paid the highest blue-collar compensation. They accepted me as a helper for the pipe fitter crew, and my goal was to become a machinist, which was a more desirable job.

This job required a keen sense of feel for measuring the thickness of metal. I went to night school at Delaware Technical Community College while working full time and studied advanced blueprint reading. I also studied machine shop equipment and learned how to operate a lathe and milling machine.

I finished my training and testing and earned the title of a professional machinist. Mechanical engineers used to approach me for machine-related issues, asking whether a part or some alteration would work on a machine.

I was offered overtime for important jobs, but I had politely stated to management that I was not interested but would take the assignment if no one else volunteered. I worked in the machine shop for maybe three years and, later on, was offered the job of foreman.

I was assigned the position of foreman for an operation area that produced nylon for sale. I was able to solve some difficult problems with the equipment because of my machinist experience. On one occasion, I purchased required quality tools for a vendor and trained them on how to measure metal and to check for concentricity. This completely solved a multi-million-dollar problem. The production machines would fail at earlier-than-designed frequencies, causing significant production failures.

I was then assigned to another operation area as a foreman due to one employee receiving a serious injury. The operator's foreman was reassigned, and I took responsibility for the injured employee. Any injury in the DuPont company was considered a serious offence. Anyone injured would be required to pay close attention to the safety rules of the company.

The injured worker had 30 years with the company, and I had a discussion with him in my office concerning the injury. I said to him, "I will be monitoring your behavior very closely." He said that he understood, and I was willing to play along with the game.

I told him, "It is not a game, and I am being closely watched due to your injury. You are on probation, and you would lose your job in six months if you don't convince me that you believe in the company safety program. I will review your position each month for the next six months."

He was a loyal employee, and he said, "I believe in the safety program with all my heart."

They then assigned me to the field maintenance organization, which handled all the craft maintenance and fabrication of equipment for the entire site. The operation had 4,200 employees, and I was the foreman and had several mechanical workers reporting to me for assignments.

I worked this job for maybe six months, and then the company had a rollback situation, and they reassigned me to the machine shop as a machinist. After about a year, I was once again made foreman.

After about three years, I was promoted to the position of group supervisor and had from six to twelve foremen reporting to me. This was a very challenging position because the actions of all these people reflected on my performance. I managed and led a team, and what the team did affected my position and leadership.

During this time, I had a group known as insulators assigned to me. One of their tasks was to remove asbestos insulation from equipment and replace it with non-asbestos insulation. We followed company procedures for the removal of asbestos. A 3M 8710 mask was the required equipment. I did not feel that the mask was adequate, so I drove to another DuPont location about 100 miles away and discussed the required equipment that their location was using for the same task. I was told by the supervisor that they had tested 3M's 8710 mask and found it did not prevent the asbestos dust from entering the body.

I returned to my location and reported my findings to my supervisor. He said, "I will pass it on for consideration." But I heard nothing about changing the procedure to the Comfo II face mask that was being used by another DuPont location for the same task.

One day, after my patience and tolerance had run dry, I challenged my supervisor and said, "Our employees are not using the best equipment for the task."

"Your job is to supervise several foremen, and if you are more interested in the safety aspects of a job, then you should seek employment at another location."

At that point, I gave up, as I had a family with four small children to support. I had no option but to surrender and go with it because of my domestic situation. Several years later, my supervisor died from asbestos. It didn't come as a shock, but as a lesson to others that when something problematic emerges in the work environment, immediately sort it out before it sorts out the ones it wants to take out.

The workforce will produce power if they are healthy. Their health affects the business the same way the business affects their health. I have a spot on my lung that has been present for the past thirty years, but it seems to be stable and does not cause me any ill effects. Fortunately, I am still running.

I was next assigned to the store material department. As an operator, if any area needed a part or supply, they would submit an electronic material request through the computer, and someone from the stores would remove the item from inventory and place it on a cart for delivery. Stores handled around 50,000 parts to support the operation. Some operators worked in inventory pulling and restocking, while others worked in ordering and receiving materials to restock the supply.

I was also given the responsibility of the purchasing department for the site at the same time. This team consisted of six people, each in a private office in the main administrative building with all the top officials of the site. The men all wore suits and ties, and the ladies wore appropriate dresses.

If someone in the store department needed to discuss an item with a purchasing agent, they had to walk from the manufacturing area to the main office building. Vendors would visit the buyers at will to share new products they were selling or for discussions that did not necessarily support the needs of the operation. I decided to close down the purchasing operation and make significant changes.

The site had five operations areas that made different products for sale. I provided an office for each buyer in the respective area they supported and closed down the main office building operation. I discontinued the allowance of vendors visiting the buyers at will. If a vendor needed to see a buyer, they first had to obtain a pass from the guardhouse.

No entrance was allowed to the site except through the guarded entrances. Needless to say, this was not viewed as a favorable move by the buyers. One of the buyers came to my office one day and said, "I want to discuss the changes you have made. I cannot do my job in an office with no windows." And then he started crying.

This was a forty-year-old man. So, I reassigned him to another job that allowed him to have more mobility. He was satisfied, although the new job did not pay quite as much as the buyer assignment.

Along with this change, I decided the foreman of the store operation added no value to the job. I developed a plan that would allow the foreman to be reassigned, and the operators would work by preset objectives. This was the first time in the company that a self-managed team was organized and proven to work well.

Each person knew their assignment well and needed few instructions. I held a weekly meeting with the group to discuss issues and they all seemed fairly happy with the change.

However, they did request background music be installed. I arranged to have the music installed with the stipulation that the music type would be changed frequently. At the same time, their supervisor had about 40 years of service. When I met him, I said, "I will be installing computers for all salaried people to conduct their business with." He informed me, "I do not want to use the computer, and I don't need it for my business."

He went on vacation the next week. I took the liberty of installing a computer in his office for him. When he returned, he was not happy with the changes in his office. "You must learn and use the computer to perform your job," I told him.

"I will not use the computer, and I have decided to retire from the company." So he retired from the company with a good pension. He just felt that learning how a computer works was too much of an effort at his age.

My next assignment was at the corporate level. The position was known as Replica Parts Coordinator. This was quite an interesting assignment. Again, my experience as a machinist came in very handy. I had the right knowledge required to manufacture different parts.

I went to the fabricating facilities that DuPont purchased parts from and studied their operations to determine if they were using the best practices to ensure DuPont was getting the best pricing. During my time, I determined that the OEM part was produced by another vendor for around half the price of the Original Equipment Manufacturer.

I had a sound background as a machinist and was well aware of the cost of fabrication. I would travel to a DuPont location and examine their purchasing records and determine the cost of individual parts or equipment. I would determine how many of these supplies were used in a year. I would find an independent machine shop that would make the part at a reduced price. If the new supplier cost was $400 each and the original equipment manufacturer charged $950 for the same part and the company used 200 per year, the saving would be $110,000 ear year. I used this same procedure on hundreds of items. Some of the items might only cost ten cents each, but I would find another supplier that would produce the items for five cents each. That was a 50% saving for several thousand parts each year. It was a very successful program used in ten locations.

The program provided a $30 million reduction in the cost of various materials and proved successful. This was a freelance project where I decided which products needed investigation. I had no restrictions on my travel and just had to provide results.

My next assignment was as a planning and scheduling supervisor. This was a completely new idea for the company. The concept was to have all requirements for maintenance of a machine that produced a product for sale provided prior to the equipment being shut down.

I had the responsibility for the entire development of this program. One of the first things to consider was the level of compensation and the need for either salaried or hourly wage people to perform this task. I developed all the procedures around this concept.

We decided to use hourly wage mechanics and upgrade them to non-exempt salaries. If they had to work extra hours, they were compensated above their normal salary. Normally, the personnel superintendent worked closely with me before a decision was made about personnel relations. After the inter-

view with a prospect was completed, the personal superintendent, area manager, and I would discuss the views provided and
make a selection. I usually had the final say and the other two
just gave the process more credibility.

People had to be selected to perform the task. I worked with
the personnel superintendent and a manager from each operational area to interview people from each operational area. We
had assigned one planner to each of the product areas, and we
had a pre-selected questionnaire developed for the candidates.
We asked each person the same basic questions to avoid any
future complications.

In one case, a college graduate applied and was interviewed
for the job, but we selected another mechanic for the job. The
college graduate was not pleased with our decision and had
some very non-complementary words to say. He expressed his
dissatisfaction after the interview with me. I accepted his criti-
cism and thanked him for participating in the interview.

We then developed a procedure to follow. The planner was
responsible for confirming that all materials needed to repair
equipment were in placed in an area that was secure and available only for the said repair. An evaluation of the time spent
procuring materials prior to the implementation of this process
indicated that approximately 30% of the mechanics time was
spent obtaining materials during the day of repairs.

The planner was also responsible for providing various personnel to perform the repair, and he had to determine how many
hours were required to make the repair. Additionally, he had to
check if necessary safety considerations were followed, and he
had to determine how many of each craft skill was required and
at what point in the repair they were required.

Next, the operational area where the repair was to be done

had to properly lockout the equipment to ensure the safety of those working on that equipment. He had to guarantee the equipment would be available at the designated time that the mechanical support personnel was to arrive.

To ensure that all parties understood their responsibilities, we held a meeting the day prior to the repair to ensure all personnel responsible for each function agreed to the timings. The planner was present and available to provide any assistance needed to make sure they accomplished the repair as planned.

All maintenance jobs were planned in advance, and a plan was established on the computer. Moreover, all jobs for an area were identified on the computer as well, and a selection was made a week prior regarding the work to be performed, ensuring that all of the planned jobs were of the proper priority. An area might have 100 jobs in the computer system. However, only a few can be selected each week due to the availability of craftsmen. All high-priority jobs were kept on the assigned list first.

I developed a method for measuring the success of the program in each area. First, I identified all the tasks required to accomplish a job by the planned method. Then I assigned a numerical value to each task. The most important task received a higher number. I identified around 40 individual tasks required to complete a routine job.

Each task would receive a number from one to ten. I would then monitor a job and assign values according to how well each task was performed. Then I would monitor each of the five production areas, and the score of the evaluation would indicate how well the areas were following the procedure.

After monitoring for several weeks, it identified both the high adherence areas and the areas needing support. This was a very accurate method of identifying compliance. It was not necessary that the assigned numbers to each task were precise, but that the same numbers were always used. The method of making repairs was then utilized throughout the corporation. I then went to another location and helped implement this concept. This was a very interesting assignment for me. I learned a lot and shared a lot with my colleagues.

My last assignment with DuPont was a corporation-level position in the engineering department, and I received a promotion to senior engineer. I was responsible for developing the maintenance computer system for 10 DuPont Fiber plants.

This assignment provided me with direct access and control of the computer code writers for the system. I developed the user specifications and provided them for the coding analysis. To provide the user specifications, I had a representative from each of the ten locations share what they would like the system to do. I then had all the reps attend a meeting, and I prioritized the interest and provided the code writers with a priority list of requirements for them to work on. I monitored them on a regular basis.

My career with DuPont was very interesting. One person that stands out as a great person to work with and a good friend over the years was Chuck Stewart from Richmond, Virginia. Chuck served as a platoon leader during the Vietnam conflict. His unit was responsible for providing bridges and roads for the troops to move on. Several of his close friends were killed during his tour, and he still kept close contact with those who were in his unit.

I believe part of my success with DuPont was that I always treated each assignment as if it was my personally owned business.

Saving Lives

Once I found myself in a situation where I had to think fast and make a move in order to save a life. The event was described in the DuPont company newspaper.

> *Jim Gardner, Maintenance Supervisor "D" shift Polymer and salt, was honored along with Donald Tull, an employee of peninsula Oil Co. as Firemen of the year by the American Legion and received a plaque commemorating the event.*
>
> *Both men were selected by the Seaford Fire Chiefs and Officers as recipients of this award for their swift action in rescuing and decisive action in rescuing and reviving an unconscious victim from a burning and smoke-filled house.*
>
> *Donning Scott Air Packs in the truck on the way to the fire, Gardner and Tull saved precious time by being able to enter the burning home immediately upon arrival at the scene. The heat was very bad, and the smoke was so thick it was difficult to see, but Gardner finally located the victim on a couch and wrapped his arm around her and proceeded to leave the home. Gardner thought she was gone. When we started to administer CPR, she had black smoke coming out of her mouth. The hospital stated that she could not have been saved if the rescue had taken another 5 minutes. It was close, Jim recalls. The victim was taken to the hos-*

pital, where her condition was considered critical due to smoke inhalation and burns.

The incident again emphasizes the necessity for quick responsive action. In the case of house fires, the policy of the Seaford Fire Department is for men to put on the Scott Air Pack on the verge to the fire. The purpose is to save precious time at the scene, as happened in this instance. Lives depend on being prepared.

The Fire department also provided ambulance service for the community. I remember once a young girl was involved in a car accident on a small road while driving a Volkswagen. The driver's side was crushed in, and it was difficult to get her out. I grabbed the seat with her in it and dislodged the seat from the car and removed her. She had some serious injuries.

A few days later, I got a call to transfer her to a major hospital for further treatment, as the local hospital did not have the facilities for the required treatment. When I arrived at the major hospital in Wilmington. Delaware, I escorted her to the emergency room for admission and I was told to just leave her, and they would see that she was transferred to a room. I stated I would not leave her alone in the emergency room to wait for her room and that I would deliver her to her room and help move her to her bed. The hospital honored my request, and I waited with her for about an hour.

Life is unpredictable. It throws you into moments where you have to act quickly. In split seconds, things can fall on this side or over the other. You just have to be prepared for whatever life throws at you. At times your decision will involve another human being. I am not scaring you, just prompting you to be prepared for anything.

Consulting Work

Consulting in China

After leaving DuPont in 1993, I was called and asked to consider a job in China. I negotiated a contract for one year with all expenses paid and I would receive $4,200 per week. I also negotiated for Rosie to go with me with all expenses paid for her. Just before we were to leave, Sharon, our daughter, had a serious cancer diagnosis and had to have a stem cell transplant procedure. Rosie decided to stay and support Sharon, so she did not go. I accepted and flew first-class to Suzhou, a city about 100 miles south of Shanghai.

My responsibility was to lead the development of the materials management section to train the leadership team in best practices. This was a joint venture in Suzhou, China. The name of the factory was DuPont Suzhou Polyester. Several other Fortune 500 companies were also invested in the venture. I was supporting the site leadership team with best practices for leading a successful business.

I was well qualified and well organized. I developed a good working relationship with the Chinese. They respected me and accepted my direction with few problems. I once led a training seminar on safety for members of the Communist Party at a grade school location. I remember the children gathered outside of the school, all in straight lines, with one person reporting that their group was ready for inspection. They all did some exercises before class. Throughout the city, most people did exercises at the beginning of the day for one-half an hour. The area where I worked was just about an open field when I started. The assignment went well for a few months.

Word got back to me that the site manager had made some disrespectful comments to another person, who was also a contractor. I went to his office and confronted him about the remarks. He said that it was a misunderstanding and that he had inquired into several operating areas I was supporting and was told that I was doing an outstanding job. I told him I did not respect him and that it was not professional for him to discuss my status or criticize me to another employee. I told him I was leaving the next day for home. He offered me a credit card and told me to take a trip over the weekend and come back on Monday and everything would be okay. I told him I was going home, and I left the next day.

While in China, I had a personal support person who accompanied me a lot when I went out. Jane was a young lady that took care of all my needs. When I told her I was leaving, she begged me to stay and asked what she could do to make me stay. We were very close, and she came to my apartment that night to again ask me to stay. I again refused, and the only romantic relationship we had was a passionate kiss goodbye. I am sure that she would have come back with me if I had asked her.

All the Chinese people were very kind to me. My Chinese sponsor once asked me to come to a meeting of about 50 managers that would be the complete leadership team of the site. As he greeted everyone, he introduced me and stated that I would lead the meeting. I had no pre-notice that I would lead the meeting.

I took the stage and told everybody that I needed five minutes to go to the bathroom. During the five minutes, I decided how

I would continue. I thought of a process that I learned at Du-Pont. I broke the group out into smaller groups and asked each group to identify how they would like their site to be and then identify what was preventing it from being that way. We then prioritized these items. Next, we identified what would have to take place to make the desired changes and assigned people to work on the issues. This was one of the toughest things I had to do as a consultant.

Consulting For Other Companies

I did consulting work with many Fortune 500 companies, including General Tire, Hood Industries, Alcoa, and several others. I worked through a company from Florida. The owner was good at sales, so he got most of the jobs. I was good at implementation and being able to show the companies the opportunities of following my recommendations. My pay was usually $2500 per week, and I had to pay the company that I worked for one half of my pay. Of course, they paid all of my expenses.

When I stopped doing the consulting work, I drove a school bus for a few years for a farmer in Queen Anne's County, Maryland. I was paid $100 for about four hours of work each day. One year, I had accumulated $10,000 in the safe just by putting the school bus money away.

I was appointed the District Court Commissioner for Caroline County, Maryland. The District court was the entry point for any criminal arrested in Caroline County, and for any police agency, including federal marshals. I worked a week on and a week off, covering the county from 5 p.m. until 8 a.m. the next day. Unless I was called by a police agency, I didn't have to leave home. Sometimes, I might not get a call. Other times, I would have to make several trips a day with very little sleep.

Late at night, I would have to decide to either put someone in jail or set bail. I would also have to accept money for bail if a bondsman or other person could raise the money. I finally resigned due to not getting any sleep for long hours on weekends.

Some of the police officers had told me they and others were saving their arrest warrants until I came on duty, as they knew I would not make them wait for a long time with somebody in their car.

Racial Relations and High School

When I was in high school, I was not that aware of race as an issue. All white kids went to white schools and Black kids went to Black schools. We thought nothing was wrong with that. Most of the adults always referred to Black people as inferior and said that they were OK as long as they stayed in their place. Black families in Caroline County, Maryland, mostly worked in low-skilled jobs and as farm and field laborers. When we worked in the same field with Black workers at a black owned farm, at lunch (dinner) the white workers ate at the dining room table and Black family workers ate in the kitchen or on the porch. If a bar or tavern served Black customers, a partition was in place so that the white people and Black people could not talk or mingle with each other. For housing, Black families had a street or section of town where they lived and white families lived in the rest of the town. In Greensboro, I never met a Black person except for Fletcher Rhyne, who owned a farm in the area. He would assist other farmers as needed, and they would all assist Fletcher as required. He was highly respected in the community. The first Black person I knew, other than Fletcher, was in the Navy. Back in the 50s, the only position on a submarine for a Black person was a cook.

Black people all lived on one side of the street. We had no interracial marriages. I really did not recognize Black people as equal until after I finished high school. First, while driving the school bus, I realized that trouble with children was not associated with color, but mostly with the environment. One Black child that lived in an affluent neighborhood was at the end of the route and he would always offer to close all the windows and caused no trouble. The bus had open seating, but the Black students always sat together and the white students in another section. The students wanted music. Usually, the Black kids wanted some rap or other hip-hop music, while the white kids wanted either country or pop.

I told them I would allow music with rap in the morning and country in the afternoon. They all seemed to accept the arrangement.

Second, when I was the District Court Commissioner in Caroline County, Maryland, the state police brought in a Black lady charged with assault. I heard the case. The lady was going to work at midnight and taking her 16-year-old son to stay with somebody, as she did not want to leave him at home. On the way, the son caused a lot of discomfort for her trying to drive the car. She smacked him in the face to gain control. I told the trooper to remove the handcuffs, and I released her for a later court date. I could make the court within a week or set it later. I gave her three months to obtain a lawyer.

Another case involving an elderly Black couple helped me understand I did not have any discrimination against Black people, even though I was raised that way. Their grandson was arrested, and they were providing bail. They did not have proper documentation for their property to set bail. Normally, I would advise the people to get proper papers and come back at another time. For them, I went to another office and found their proper papers and made copies so that they could raise bail. These examples allowed me to see that even though I was raised in a segregated community, I always treated Black people with disregard for their color.

High School Years

My whole graduation class had about 25 students. One night some of us guys, most of us around 16 years old, had nothing to do, so we created our own entertainment. We saw the chassis of a car at the repair shop about a half mile from the river. We decided to push it into the water at the bridge across the Choptank River at Greensboro, Maryland. The next day I was riding the school bus to school and saw many people at the river with a wrecker pulling the car from the river.

We never did things to hurt people but would do things that were generally accepted as innocent fun in those days. One night, we stole a pig and went to the woods to cook it for something to eat. Another boy and I decided that it was not the right thing to do. So, we loaded the pig in the back seat of the car and took it back to the owner's pig pen and let it loose.

We used to play poker sometimes after school at my friend Gale Nashold's house. We did not have money, so we played for cigarettes or toothpicks.

I used to enjoy shop in school and made a few things that I still have today. A little wooden centerpiece is still on my table. I did not have girlfriends in high school, but I did date some of my classmates after graduation. I was normally just a little shy and afraid of being turned down. I used to enjoy going to country music dancing at the Hitching Rail dance hall on the Denton-Easton Road. I met some girls there and did date some of them.

I really did not like school and did not apply myself much. It took me a few years to understand that I was a quick learner and that I normally could finish any learning experience at the top of the class. After I graduated from high school, I went to college at nighttime while working at DuPont and always finished at the top, even though I was in my early 40s and most of the other students were in their late teens. I did exceptionally well in college accounting, money and banking, and human relations courses. I think I earned around 34 credits. During my working career, I tried to constantly improve myself. I took college level English, accounting, and banking courses. I also earned my real estate license at Wesley College in Dover, Delaware.

Things We Did Not Have in 40s and 50s

There wasn't much modern technology when we were growing up. Things we take for granted today just weren't a part of our lives back then. Here's a look at things that just didn't exist then.

No Cell Phones

We got our first home phone around 1950. It was a party line with five people on the same line, and you could pick up your phone and listen to your neighbor talk. You would hear a click when someone picked up their phone to listen to your conversation. I remember my mom hearing the click, so she called them by name and told them to get off the phone until she finished her call.

No Computers

No CDs, DVRs, cassettes, or tape players. The big thing was 78 rpm records. We got 45 rpm records in the mid-50s. They might have been available a little while before that. I sent Rosie an Elvis Presley 45 rpm record that I bought in the Navy store. I know we bought many 33 rpm records in the 60s before the small cassette became available.

No TV

Television became available to the public around 1950, and we got our first one around 1958. We had a radio that did not play too well. During the 40s, we had to have a lamp with a bottom light on the floor so that we could turn all the lights off in case of an air raid during the war.

No McDonald's or Other Fast-Food Restaurants

If you wanted some light food, each town had a small restaurant. Baltimore had the first fast food place that I heard of. It was known as White Castle and sold five hamburgers for $1.00.

No Bridge Across the Chesapeake Bay

You had to take a ferryboat ride for an hour to get to go west to Baltimore, south to Norfolk.

Many local roads were dirt without pavement. If you traveled during a rainstorm, you probably had to drive on a muddy road and sometime the car would get stuck.

Walking to town and other places was normal for many people who could not afford a car. Some people would hitch-hike, and it was considered safe to accept a ride from a stranger. I know that sometimes I had time off for a few days while I was in the Navy and would hitchhike several hundred miles to get home for a couple of days.

No Electric Refrigerator

During the 40s and early 50s, we had an icebox to keep the food cool. We had to get a block of ice every couple of days. During the winter, we would collect snow and make a snow cone to use as ice cream.

No Multiscreen Movie Theaters

Most towns had one movie house. In the 50s, movies normally cost about 25 cents. You could go on Saturday afternoon for five cents and get a candy bar for five cents. I think Necco wafers were the best buy for candy. You could get about 50 round pieces of candy for five cents.

Married and Raising Children

I married my first true love on December 17, 1960. We had dated for a couple of years before that. Rosie was 18, and I was 22 when we married. I had been discharged from the Navy on November 26, and went back to work at DuPont on December 1. We had no money and no savings and no place to live. At our wedding reception, we got a couple of hundred dollars and that was what we had and maybe one check from DuPont for working. We rented a furnished apartment in Seaford for $15.00 a week, payable each Saturday by noon time.

We had a wonderful honeymoon and went as far south as Natural Bridge, Virginia. I think I only had $20.00 left, so we

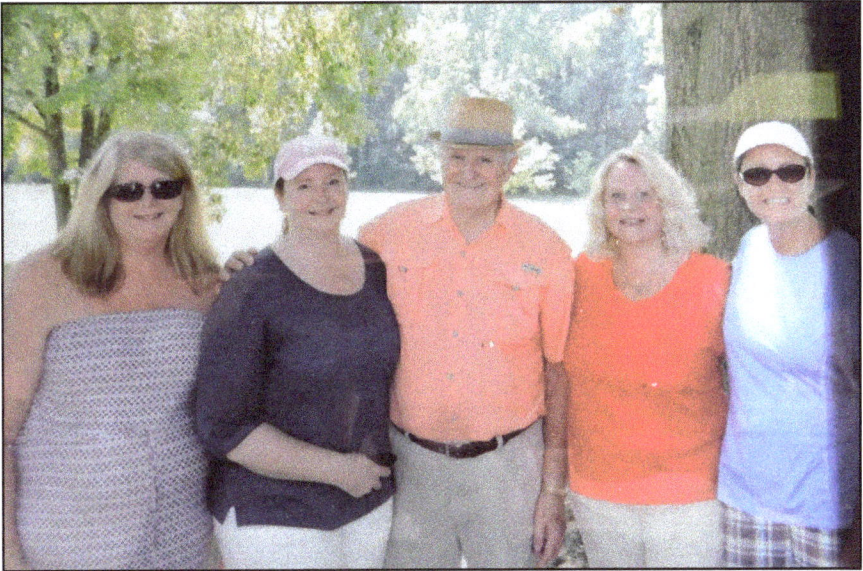

The author, Jim Gardner, and his daughters

headed home in a heavy snowstorm. The muffler came loose on the car and was dragging the road. I stopped at a filling station, and they fixed it for me for nothing. When we got home, we had $2.53 left to live on. We bought a package of cheap lunch meat for 30 cents and some bread.

One time in the early 60s, rockfish were very plentiful and could be bought for five cents a pound. We ate a lot of rockfish. We just lived on love for the rest of the week. For some time, I took a sandwich consisting of one slice of meat and two slices of bread, and five cents to get a cup of coffee. We normally went to her folks' and my folks' place on weekends to get some good meals.

Rosie had never had a bathroom at home, so when I came home from working the 4 to 12 shift, she would normally be soaking in the bathtub.

Bee Tree Road

LIFE AT BEE TREE: 1993 – 2004

After retiring from DuPont in March 1993 with 37 years of service, we decided to build a new home close to Rosie's father on the old family farm. Rosie's grandfather bought the farm, and when he died, it went to her father. We were given ten acres of land to build on and were told that this was Rosie's inheritance from her father. Her only brother, Carl, was given the farm which was about 60 acres with a home and outbuildings. We did not have an issue with this at the time or any time afterward.

Her father stated openly that he thought that money was wasted on a girl and that the male was the important one. Rosie knew this, but always treated her father with full love and respect. She cared for her mother during her cancer treatment and other illnesses and after her death, did the laundry and had her father come to our house every week for dinner. She always prepared meals for him to take home for the following week.

Her father usually treated me with respect, but he told another family member and it got back to me that "Jim should not expect anything or money from me while he is building his house because I will not give him anything."

We built a really nice rancher with two bedrooms. After two or three years, we decided we needed more room, so I added another large section. I then built Rosie a little garden building that was for her exclusive use for her garden tools. Next, we built a 24- by 30-foot garage and workshop. After that, we purchased a new Winnebago motor home, so I built a large, tall building to house the motor home.

I did all the construction, including the electrical work myself. I bought the surrounding woods and some other adjoining land to finally have 100 acres. My friends would visit in the fall and winter, and we would have a good deer hunting association. We finally sold the property in 2004 for around $400,000, which gave us enough money to build another new home for $200,000, which we lived in for ten years. We sold that for $258,000, so we made a little on that one. I bought a home in a gated community for $127,000 and sold it after Rosie's death for $158,000. So, I have had pretty good results on my homes.

TYE PRUITT

I met Tye when I lived on my farm on Bee Tree Road, in Henderson, Maryland. I used to enjoy stopping by his farm only a couple of miles from my place. He was in his early 80s when I met him. He was a very pleasant man that enjoyed helping underprivileged people, and he expected nothing in return. I have several stories to relate as to what kind of a man he was.

First, he told me about how he met his wife in North Carolina. I think it was in the Charlotte area. In the late 30s, he would go to Charlotte each year and buy a new Cadillac. He was riding on a country road and noticed a pretty young girl, maybe 15- or 16-years old, picking cotton in the field. He said to himself that he thought she might make a good wife. He turned around and went up to the house and spoke to the mother. He said he would like to marry her and that he could provide well for her.

He said that he would be back in December, and they agreed she could go with him and be his wife. He came back, and they were married and moved to his farm in Henderson, Maryland.

He said they were happily married for nearly 60 years until

she passed away. After she passed, he hired a housekeeper to clean and cook for him. She was a young girl in her mid-20s. She had worked for a while, and he was not satisfied with how she kept the house clean. She had a boyfriend who would visit her sometimes in the evenings.

On one evening, as the boyfriend was getting ready to leave, Tye was watching TV in the living room and the boyfriend came to him and said that he knew that Tye always carried some money with him. He told Tye that he was going to take his money and that he would not hurt him unless he put up some resistance. He grabbed Tye, and Tye tried to protect himself. They struggled, and as Tye fell to the floor, he pulled his .38 out of his pocket and killed the guy. There was an investigation, and it was decided that Tye was only defending himself. No charges were ever filed against him.

At that time, he was a sizable bootlegger in Caroline County, Maryland. He said he made great whiskey. He would put ten one-gallon containers of whiskey in the trunk of his car and head for the Kennedy estate in Massachusetts. When he got to the state line in Marydel, Maryland, a Delaware State Police officer would escort him to the next state. He had a police escort through each state until he got there. He knew the Kennedy family.

On one occasion, he had a lot of whiskey made and ready to ship. His still was located well within a wooded area. It snowed a lot that day and the previous night. Tye decided to check on his whiskey supply. He noticed that one container full of whiskey was missing. He noticed some tracks in the snow leading away from his supply.

He walked in deep snow for two or three hours and came up to the end of the tracks at a neighbor's house. He said he turned around and went back home and did not mention it to the person. He just wanted to know who it was and said that he would keep it in his mind for the rest of his life.

Later, he was arrested for bootlegging and spent time in federal prison. After he served his time, he was told that if he ever owned property, the government would take it for the crime he committed. He owned several farms and always put them in the name of Wilmer Mitchell, his son born out of wedlock.

I owned around 100 acres on Bee Tree Road, about two miles from Tye's farm. About half of it was wooded and good for deer hunting. Just about everybody in that part of the county enjoyed deer hunting. I also grew beans in a field that required combining. Tye had a combine and would cut a farmer's beans for a certain fee per acre. I used to hire him to cut beans. His son, Wilber, would drive the combine.

One year it was very dry, and the crop was very poor. After we harvested my beans, Tye came by one day for his payment. He knew that I hardly made any money on the beans that year, so he cut my fee in half and said that was all he needed to cover his expenses. He was a good man.

Mr. Trimmer

I built my new home on Bee Tree Road, and a little home (shack) was located nearby. Mr. Trimmer lived there alone with his dog and horse. He would ride his horse three or four miles to a local store to get what supplies he needed. Tye stopped by Mr. Trimmer's house one day and asked if he could hunt squirrels. Mr. Trimmer gave him permission, and Tye went to the woods and laid back against a large oak tree. He shot two squirrels and gave one to Mr. Trimmer. He thanked Mr. Trimmer and had to go to the store for some things. When he got to the store, he found out that his wallet was missing. He had several hundred dollars in it. He stopped by Mr. Trimmer's on the way home and did not say anything about losing his wallet. As he was leaving, Mr. Trimmer handed him his wallet and told him he was walking in the woods and saw it by the tree.

Tye offered to give him a reward for his honesty, but Mr. Trimmer refused to accept.

A few days later, he was passing Mr. Trimmer's house and noticed his horse was down in the field. He went to Mr. Trimmer and asked him about the horse. He was told that the horse had just died. Tye said goodbye and left. He went straight to the animal yard that sells horses and bought a horse for Mr. Trimmer and had it delivered and had the dead horse removed. He purchased feed for the horse every month until Mr. Trimmer died. He was a good, considerate man.

Tom Thornton

Tom Thornton was the mail delivery person for Henderson, Maryland. He was a neighbor and a good friend. Tom's father was the mail carrier until he died. Tom applied for the job and was hired when he was in his early 20s. Tom would deliver mail until around 2 p.m. and then go to work on a house that he was building. He normally worked alone and could build two or three houses each year. With just a high school education, Tom was able to accumulate considerable wealth by working hard and providing a quality home. Tom's mother was a nurse and very good lady. Each spring, she would make the best zucchini quiche. It was always fresh out of the oven. Tom would always be available to help with things on the farm; he also allowed me to hunt on his property. After I built my home next to him, I decided to add a large section. Tom agreed to help me with the addition and was an excellent carpenter. He usually had all the latest news about the neighborhood.

CRABBING ON THE BAY

I had a commercial fishing and crabbing license for the Chesapeake Bay for several years. I mostly enjoyed crabbing from Easton Point in Easton, Maryland. I remember a couple of special occasions of crabbing. One morning, just as the sun was coming up, I had my lines in the water, but the crabs were not biting. I decided to look at another location. I sailed my boat up a creek to check it out. Upon getting further up the creek, I noticed another boat that was just sitting still. I pulled up within a few yards and noticed a gentleman on the bow looking out. I commented it was really peaceful just to enjoy the beginning of the day, even though the crabs weren't biting. He agreed. I had a couple of apples with me, and I asked if he would like one. He said that he sure would. I threw him one, and we just sat there and ate the apples and had small talk. I wished him a good day and said goodbye. He thanked me and wished me a good day. I just started my engine and moved out of the creek and back to my area.

On another occasion, I had my daughter Dorothy and her two sons, Mitch and Gabe, with me on the same body of water. We were crabbing in an area known as Strawberry Point and the crabs were plentiful. I was dipping the crabs and Dorothy was putting them in the baskets. I was dipping so fast that on one occasion I missed throwing the crabs in the basket and several crabs landed on her head.

I also had many enjoyable crabbing trips with two of my good friends, Joe Little and Dinky Scurto. We crabbed together and sometimes we shared one boat, and other times we were each in our own boat and just crabbed close to each other. Joe and Dink and I also enjoyed many years of deer hunting together. Both Joe and I had plenty of woods for hunting and always enjoyed hunting with Dink. We used both a firearm, and a bow and arrow, for hunting.

A few times, a friend from Rehoboth Beach, Delaware, would hunt with us. Nick owned a pizza restaurant at the beach and was the inventor of the "Nicoboli" sandwich, which he shipped all over the country. Thanksgiving day was usually the first day we would go rabbit hunting, as Joe Little had excellent dogs for rabbit hunting.

Navy Life

My life has been interesting. I have looked at the world from different angles, enjoyed a variety of experiences, and witnessed many events. One of the most interesting periods of time was my time in the Navy.

I joined the Navy in 1956 and received my honorable discharge in 1962. I would say that the experience was phenomenal, but I would advise that it is only for the fit-minded. What I mean by fit-minded is that the person beginning this journey should have not only patience, but ardent belief in their strength. This place might indeed break you, but it will mold you into a better shape.

I finished boot camp in Banbridge, Maryland. During the winter, it was usually very cold. We had to get up at 5 a.m. sharp and stand in line on a cement pad waiting to eat. Sometimes it was snowing or raining, but that was something they forced us to do. They assigned me as a recruit petty officer in charge of some activities of the other recruits. After boot camp, I went to morse code school and became a professional at using morse code.

Then I was assigned to the USS William M. Wood (DDR-715), which was a guided-missile destroyer. This was a development program to perfect the Regulus guided missile. In the beginning, it could only travel about 200 miles with guidance from one ship and then another ship 200 miles away would pick up the guidance for another 200 miles.

The Regulas was the first guided missel for use on ships and

caption?

later on submarines. And believe me when I say that I have experienced some of the very rough seas on the William M. Wood. Once we were caught in a hurricane off Cape Hatteras, and the ship lost its radar. We stayed lost in the storm for two days. When it was light again, we saw one of the ship's side panels was missing. You could hear the propellers turning out of the water.

Once we were hit on the side by a giant wave and it threw me out of my rack. I was able to grab the structural steel above my rack, but when I lowered myself down, I was in two inches of water. That was scary!

After serving aboard the William M. Wood, I volunteered for a 12-week long submarine school in New London, Connecticut, and was accepted. They accepted only about five percent of the sailors because of the physical and mental requirements.

During that school, we had to escape from a 100-foot-deep tank full of water. At 100 feet deep, the pressure on the lungs is 44 pounds per square inch. We had our lungs pressurized at 44 pounds and entered the tank from a bottom chamber. As we ascended to the top of the tank, we had to breathe out our mouth as the air in our lungs had to equalize with the pressure in the water. We had a diver with us with a balloon that was pressurized at 44 pounds. The air was not equalized in the balloon as we went up. At the top, the balloon had expanded to about two feet in diameter. The goal was to demonstrate to us what would happen to our lungs if we did not exhale.

After sub school, I was assigned to the USS Medregal (SS-480). On that submarine, I was a radio operator while we were on the surface, and performed sonar duty while we were under. I could tell the size of a ship and whether it was loaded or empty by the sound of the screws (propellers).

After being on board for six months, I took the test to qualify to continue serving on a submarine. I had to draw the complete submarine on paper with all the tanks and valves and answer any question the officer might ask. I passed the testing and got my dolphins. A sailor can only wear dolphins on his uniform after he is qualified on a submarine by an officer. Qualification was a requirement to serve on a submarine. Each person had to be proficient in his primary skill, but also be able to perform any other skill required in an emergency. I was a radio operator while we were on the surface and would perform the sonar watch when we dived. After a while, I could tell the characteristics of a ship just by the sound of the propellers.

We spent a lot of time at sea. The Medregal nearly sunk twice while I was onboard. One time, the bow planes got jammed, and we went down to over 600 feet. The test depth of this old

World War II sub was 412 feet, so the water was coming into the boat through the hull connection. The captain finally blew water from a safety tank, and we came back up to the surface and shot backward out of the water. The second time was when we came into the post, and they started the engines before air-flow was open in the boat. The hydrogen content rose to over five percent due to the batteries charging, which would blow up the ship if a match was struck. A large vacuum developed inside, and it was decided that we had to unlock a sealed door to allow fresh air. Someone on the other side of the door had their eardrums burst.

Once we had been at sea for several weeks and a plane was to bring a mail bag and drop it close to the sub and we would retrieve the bag and distribute the mail. The chief of the boat asked if anyone would dive over and get the mail. The water was pretty rough, but I agreed to get the mailbag. I only had to swim about 100 yards, but sharks were swimming around in this water off Cuba. I got the bag and swam back. The only problem was that the water was so rough that I could not grab the side of the sub to get back on board. I finally was able to grab the side as the sub was going up on a wave and I was going down on another. The captain saw this and made a new rule that no one could go off the side of the boat at sea without a rope tied to the sub.

After two close encounters on the Medregal, I transferred to the USS Spikefish (SS-404). It was a stable sub, and I was on board when we were the first sub in the world to make 10,000 dives.

I spend most of my time on sea duty in the south Atlantic, near South America, and up to the North Atlantic. I was in some very horrible storms at sea. On one occasion, we were in the

North Atlantic, and it was very rough. The captain ordered me to send a message to Washington saying that we had to dive in rough water and report what time we expected to be on the surface again. If I did not send a new message within one hour of the time they expected us to surface, the Navy would send out a rescue ship to find us. I finally got somebody in the Panama Canal zone to accept the message and send it on to Washington. We dove to 200 feet, but the sea was still active and causing the boat to sway from side to side.

It was so cold sailing in the North Atlantic. We were with no heat on the sub, and all of my fingers on both hands froze in a curled-up position and pained me very much. I tried to straighten them out, and they would just curl back up again. The captain ordered the corpsman to open a case of whiskey and give each of us two small bottles of whiskey. It seemed to help the pain some.

Other times we would be in war games and would have to stay in our rack at all times unless on duty. I think we had four hours on duty and eight hours off. We did not know if it was day or night. We could not wash any part of our body for weeks at a time. We only had three changes of underwear, as our total personal space was probably about two- or three–square feet. We put our dress clothing under our bunk and sleep on them.

I remember once that we were allowed to take a shower at sea. We were in the Caribbean Sea, and it was hot. We had no AC so our bunk would be soaked from sweating while we slept. We all went up on top of the sub where a pipe sucked in ocean water to allow us to wash some of the smell off our bodies. Within five minutes after we washed, we could actually rub our body and see a steady stream of salt falling as the water was extremely salty. We put the same underwear and clothing back on that we had been wearing for several weeks. I guess this is probably enough about the submarine duty.

While on the Spikefish, I had liberty on nearly all the Virgin Islands, and Cuba before it was closed to visitors. Normally, we would have to get permission from the harbormaster to enter port. Some islands did not have water deep enough to allow a submarine to enter. In that case, a small boat with a small motor would come out to the submarine, and about ten of us at a time could go ashore.

On St. Thomas, they did not have a great power system. I remember on one occasion we were in a bar drinking warm beer, as they had little refrigeration, and the lights went out slowly. We were told the engine that drove the generator for power had just run out of fuel. After a few minutes, the lights would slowly come back on. Most of these islands were not well developed in the 50s. However, Jamaica had a large aluminum factory and a large gambling casino and airport. I suppose many people from the USA flew to Jamaica for a weekend of gambling. Nearly all the islands had beautiful beaches.

Early Life and Childhood

I was born on July 29th, 1938, in Greensboro, Maryland. My father and mother lived in a rented house about two or three blocks from the railroad on the main street going to the station. They moved to a 70-acre farm on Knife Box Road the year after I was born. Doctor Stonesifer, a local town doctor, delivered me. He charged $4.00, and my parents did not have the money to pay him. I remember my mother telling me around 1954 that she had just paid the doctor for my birth that year, which can easily show where we stood with our monetary situation.

My mother was a registered nurse with a business degree from Goldie Beacon College in Wilmington, Delaware, and a nursing degree from Temple University in Philadelphia.

My Mother and Father

My father was a carpenter and a truck farmer. He would take a pickup load of vegetables to Wilmington with his father on Tuesday and Saturday. During the war, he always came home with a 100-pound bag of sugar or something else that was rationed during the war. My father also had a two-wheeled saw machine with a 36 Chevy engine attached to cut tree logs into firewood length for burning in a stove in the house.

Most homes were heated with wood and had a wood stove to cook with. A tank was attached to the side of the stove for heating hot water. My father would pull the saw machine to different farms and saw the winter supply of wood for a fee.

As a child, I was the youngest male, with one sister younger and a sister and brother older. The family had more means earlier, so the older two had better provisions. When I was young, I used small wooden blocks as toy trucks and pushed them on the ground. I never had a new bike and only had one used bike in poor condition with no fenders. I don't think it lasted very long. We had very little money, so we got very few presents at Christmas or Easter. One year I got a yo-yo, and another year I got a cap gun. For Easter, we got only jellybeans. I don't ever remember getting hugs or kisses as a young child. I don't even remember ever getting held by my mother or father. Many times, we had very little food. I remember having potato soup with onions as a flavoring and no meat.

We had no indoor bathroom, so we had to go outside to do our business, and we used paper from the Sears Roebuck catalog to wipe on. We tried to use the softer pages first. If we had no paper, we would use a corn cob.

My mother worked as a nurse in hospitals in Easton, Maryland, and Milford, Delaware, and took care of her four children at home. My father worked as a carpenter during the day and enjoyed his beer at a tavern during the evening.

I remember waiting on the front porch many Saturday nights to go to town for shopping, as Saturday was usually the only time we got to go.

Father would not come home until after the stores had closed, and I would hear the car with the busted muffler come up the lane late at night. Sometimes, I would hear my father and mother fussing, or mostly my mother would not wake up. Life takes on a strange color when you don't have the proper measures to go through it. It turns your body cold even when it is thirty degrees outside.

We nearly always went to church on Sunday mornings. If we were good in church, we got a treat of a nickel ice cream cone at the double-dip store in Denton. At times we kids misbehaved in church. One particular time, we misbehaved, and my mother decided to teach us a lesson. She went into our bedrooms the next Sunday and pulled the covers back and gave us a whipping with a tree branch. She said, "I just wanted to remind you to behave in the church today."

Sometimes we would go to my Uncle Mike Kibler's house on a Sunday evening for the adults to play cards. He and my aunt played pinochle. I can't remember when I did not know how to play the game as they allowed us to stand by the table and watch as long as we did not talk, including asking a question. Later in the evening, we would be given a graham cracker as a snack.

At 8 o'clock, the card game would stop, and they would turn the radio on to hear the news of the world, and we would get the news about the second world war. It was like a ritual to listen to Walter Winchell, as they considered him the absolute authority on the news of the war.

In the spring, we would plant a garden for food. My Uncle Bill had a horse, so we would borrow the horse to plow the garden with a one-horse walk-behind plow. We would usually have a normal garden with lots of potatoes and beans and some tomatoes. My father did a lot of truck farming. He raised cantaloupes, tobacco, beans, cucumbers, and tomatoes. He would take it to market in Wilmington on Saturdays. A little later, he bought a small "A" Farmall tractor, and I tilled the ground, and he planted some corn or soybeans.

At home, we would sometimes play a game called canasta with cards or monopoly. We also had some Chinese checkers and a few tinker toys. Another game we played was pick-up sticks. A bunch of small sticks were thrown in a pile, and the objective was to see how many you could pick up while tossing a small ball in the air and catching it. Sometimes I would play rummy with my grandfather, especially just prior to his death. Generally, children did not start a conversation with their grandparents. You could talk if they started the conversation, but they rarely did.

I can remember one night coon hunting and it was very cold out. My grandfather and I were listening to the dogs in his truck alongside the road. He was in good physical shape, a big man, but very kind. He couldn't walk through the woods because of his size, so he would listen to the dogs and drive the truck around the dirt roads and get out and determine how close the dogs were to the coons by the way they barked.

We got out, and it was really cold. I told him how cold my hands were. He told me to rub them together really fast and that they would warm up. I remembered that for 70 years.

In the early 1900s, my grandfather owned and operated a power plant at Garland Lake in Caroline county. This was a small operation and powered by a water wheel. I think he only ran it for a couple of years.

My mother had most of the responsibility for raising us. My father's approach was to just give us a whipping whenever necessary. I started hunting with a 16-gauge shotgun when I was around nine years old, and my hunting target would be mostly squirrels and sometimes small birds.

We would nearly always have an excellent Sunday dinner. Mother could make something good out of just about anything. I remember standing close to the wood stove on a chilly morning, and my mother was fixing hot chocolate on the stove. It really warmed you up. In the spring, the cow would eat the new grass, and the milk in the chocolate milk would have a grassy taste. I was responsible for milking the cow in the morning and sometimes in the evening in freezing conditions. The cat would stand pretty close to me, and I would squirt some milk into its mouth.

Normally, the stove would go out at nighttime and would have to be restarted in the morning in order to cook breakfast. It was also very important to trip the pump before going to bed. The water pump was in the house, but the inside of the house would freeze at night, and if we did not trip the pump, the water would freeze, and you could not get water. It was always important to get some wood inside the house in the evening in case it rained at night.

I remember one incident in my life that relates to my father. I call it the "Potsie's Snack Bar Incident". One day in 1957, I had just entered the Navy and came home for a short leave. We went to a small snack bar and was in a line of maybe 10 people. Two young men, maybe 25 years old, came in and went to the front of the line and, in a loud voice, stated they wanted service.

The waitress said that she would get to them shortly, but they said that they wanted service now. My father was around 55 years old back then. He grabbed one of them and hit him so hard that he slid 12 feet across the floor with blood streaming out of his mouth. Father then grabbed the other guy and asked him if he wanted some of the same. The second guy said no. Father then sat him on a stool and told him to wait his turn. My father was an unpredictable man. He never missed the chance of whipping people, be it his kids or strangers.

I remember on Christmas Eve we were waiting to go to midnight Mass. Finally, late at night, my father came home. He had totally wrecked the family panel truck coming home from a bar.

I would wait for my father to come home on Saturday night so that we could go to town and get groceries. I keep waiting on the front porch, looking towards town, listening for the car with no muffler. He never came that night or many other nights until after the stores closed.

I also remember once that he was putting a roof on a house and the fire alarm went off. He came off the roof and got ready to respond to the alarm. The owner of the house told him he could not go and that he had to continue working on the roof. He told the guy that he was going to the fire and that he would get somebody else to finish if he wanted to.

I would like to share several things that happened during my early life that seem to stand out. Deer hunting was introduced in Caroline County around 1949. That's when I saw a deer for the first time up close. I was about six feet from it. I was on the edge of a field, and it was just inside of the woods. I was walking along the edge of the woods quietly, and l looked in the woods and saw a big doe. I pulled up the gun and looked at her for a while, then I lowered the gun, and she ran off. She was too pretty to shoot.

During the winter, I enjoyed ice skating with friends. Many of the farms would have a little low spot of maybe an acre. It would freeze over in late December, and we could skate until late February. We used to skate on a large lake at the beginning of the Choptank River. We could build a fire on the edge of the ice and really enjoy skating.

My cousins and I would walk along all the wood's long roads during the summer and swim in the local streams whenever we could. I remember once the older guys encouraged me to dive off a bridge into a stream. I thought it might not be too deep, but they assured me it was deep. The water was two feet deep, but I dove from eight feet. I really cut up my hands and face when I hit the water and scraped the bottom. I still have scars.

We used to do what is now known as waterboarding. Two people would hold your hands and feet and put your head underwater and see how long you could stay without drowning. It might sound strange and dangerous, but we did it for the thrill.

My hobbies for most of my life revolved around gardening, woodworking, hunting, growing grapes, and making wine. I always had a splendid vegetable garden, even when I lived in a town with a small lot in the backyard. I always grew enough to give away to neighbors.

Sweet corn is best when eaten just after pulling. If we were having corn for dinner, my wife, Rosie, would put the water on to boil, and I would pull the corn. It was ready to eat 30 minutes after pulling. I grew all the other garden things, including watermelons, cantaloupes, and honeydew.

I planted my grape vines and usually had grapes for wine within two years. Winemaking is a science but also a skill. I had a grinder for grinding several baskets of grapes. I also had a wine press to press the grapes after they set in a barrel for seven days. Next, the wine was drained and put into five-gallon bottles with a seal and hose going into a water jug.

A little yeast will help it begin. After 8 to 10 weeks, it will probably stop working with no bubbles visible. We can then bottle it into smaller bottles. This is just a basic winemaking procedure. Many other things must be considered to make good wine. I usually made a dark wine with concord grapes and was well known in my community for making excellent wine. Gardening was like therapy for me. I enjoyed doing it and sharing the stuff I grew with people around me.

Life on the Farm

We had very little food to spare for the dog and cat we had on the farm. Our dog would usually hunt rabbits, and sometimes when I was milking the cow, the cat would come close to where I was milking, and I would squirt milk into her open mouth.

Once, we had a pretty black dog that somebody had dropped close to our house, and he came to our place to get food. We just did not have enough food for this dog and our dog. My father told me to take the 12-gauge shotgun and take the dog for a walk in the woods. The dog seemed to like me, so it was no problem getting it to follow me. When I got about halfway to the woods, I hollered at the dog to make it get away from me. I took aim and shot the dog. I buried him, but never forgot the feeling of having to shoot something that I really liked. I had no choice. A kid had to do what he was told to do or suffer the belt.

We mostly had to make our own fun in any way we could. I remember one of my favorite toys was a wagon wheel with a stick through the center hole of the wheel and a nail on each side so that the stick would not come out. I would just run beside it with the stick in my hand and roll the wheel.

We did not have a telephone until around 1955. If I wanted to meet with a cousin, I would just stand on the porch and yodel real loud. If somebody answered, you would meet and find something to do.

I used to like to run, and sometimes I would meet my cousin, Michael Kibler, and we would run a couple of miles to school in the morning. Michael was a good boy, but he did not have even as much as we had. He was born out of wedlock, as were his eight or nine brothers and sisters. He was a good boy and a good friend of mine.

I remember one cold night when we heard somebody outside hollering for us to get up. They said, "Mom is ready." Mother would get up and go across the field about a half mile and deliver a baby for Aunt Vode, the wife of my Uncle Jonny. Nearly all of the people in the community were related.

My father would hire me out to other farmers to cultivate tomatoes since we had a side attachment to fertilize the crops. I would receive none of the money. Tomato fields were only three or four acres. Many farmers raised large crops of maybe 50 to 75 acres of sweet corn or beans.

Back in the 50s, we had no mechanical method of harvesting the crops. When it was time to harvest, a team of two horses would pull a wagon down the center row of corn, and four people would each take two rows of corn and cut the corn off with a machete and throw it in the wagon.

The animals pulled the wagon at a steady pace without a driver, and we were expected to keep up with our two rows. When the wagon was full, we would throw each bunch of corn onto a truck to take to the packing house. After the corn was removed from the husk, it was processed, and the husk loaded back on the truck as silage for the animals to eat in the wintertime.

We had to put the silage into a tall cylinder tank that was maybe 25 feet in diameter and 40 feet high. A machine would keep filling the tank, and two of us would be inside the tank, starting at the bottom and making the silage level until we got to the top of the tank. When the tank was full, we would crawl out of the top of the tank and climb down to the bottom. One good thing about working on the farm was that they fed us well.

My Uncle Charles Ellwanger was an exception. When I worked for him, he paid me 50 cents an hour, and we had only 30 minutes for lunch. They counted the 30 minutes from the time the equipment stopped until it started up again.

All the walking and getting positioned at the table was part of the 30 minutes. He was not very kind to me. I remember one day when I was maybe 15 or 16 years old. I was stacking hay bales on a wagon as he drove the bailer. We had worked for maybe two or three hours without stopping. My throat was so dry that I could hardly swallow. We always had a gallon jug of water in the milk house by the barn. I asked him to stop for a minute so that I could get a drink of water. He did not stop. He hollered to me, saying we would be finished in a while and that I could get a drink then.

I loaded the wagons alone. After the hay was loaded and the wagons were at the barn, my uncle would get additional help to put the hay in the barn. The easy job was to drop the bales from the wagon onto the conveyor belt that took them to the barn loft.

He always assigned me to go to the loft, which was very hot and dusty as the air had no way to circulate. I would never get a break as the two on the wagon could always drop more bales on the conveyor than I could arrange in a stacked position in the loft.

My Uncle Charles was a very wealthy farmer in Caroline County, owning 1,000 acres of farmland, and was also a director of the Denton National Bank.

Another farmer that I helped a lot was Bill Harper. He had little money, but he bought his own farm and was a good farmer. He lost a kidney when he was probably only around 30 years. He would pay me $5.00 to work on a Saturday for him.

In the spring, I would plow the fields and cultivate and harvest the crops. In the winter, he would give me odd jobs, and one of them was very dirty. I would clean all the cow manure from the pound area. It was normally very wet and cold. I would load the manure on a spreader, and when the spreader was full, I would drive a tractor to the fields and spread the manure.

One day it was raining, and the temperature was 34 degrees. I arrived and went to the pound and started loading the spreader with a pitchfork. I did not have boots but had only old sneakers with holes in the side of them. He came up to me and stopped me from working. He handed me $5.00 and told me to go home. He said that it was not fit for anybody to be working outside in these conditions. I could never forget him.

Later in life, after he had died, I had been appointed District Court Commissioner for Caroline County, Maryland, and one day the State Police brought in a person for violating a restraining order. I heard the case and decided that the person was set up and that he did not intentionally violate the order. He happened to be Bill Harper's son. I told the police to take off the handcuffs and release him on his own recognizance. I told him he could thank his father.

Bill Harper married a little late in life. The lady he married had been married a couple of times and sometimes enjoyed visiting a bar. Some of the neighbors looked down on her, but to me, she was a great lady. She always had a Thanksgiving dinner for me when I worked at the farm on that day, even if I was the only one working. Any time I ever heard anybody make any remarks about her that were not complimentary, I would always speak my piece about how much I respected her.

When we finished eating, Bill would have to rest for half an hour since he had only one kidney. I would get up and start out the door to get back to work. He would tell me to go lay under the tree for a while and let my food settle. He said that he would tell me when it was time to go back to work. What a thoughtful man he was. For a young boy that had nothing, the only spending money I would have would be what he shared with me. Some people remain with you even when they leave. Their kindness exceeds the limit of their body.

I always did well in school, but I was also a jokester. I did not understand English very well and rarely did well in English. I did extremely well in math and algebra, and I was the best student in algebra. Most of the popular boys and I goofed off after the ninth grade. It was probably a waste of taxpayers' money for us to go to school. I did well in sports except for baseball. They put me in the catcher's position, and I was afraid of the ball and could not see it coming. We did not have football. We only had basketball, soccer, and baseball. I was told by my algebra teacher, Mr. Barrett, that I should try to get a job in the math field as I would do well. Mr. Barrett (math and algebra) and Mr. Duffee (sports teacher) were my favorite teachers.

I graduated by taking a lead part in the year's class play. Mrs. Hastings, the English teacher, said she would fail me if I did not accept the lead part in the yearly play, which she directed. Her husband was the principal. I did not respect him, and we did not get along.

Being Catholic in a heavily Protestant community had its problems. I did not realize how much we were discriminated against until later in life and I looked back on things. Normally, the town would have a cotillion dance to recognize the proper teenagers in the community. The dance was organized by the community leaders. I was never invited, but just thought it was because I did not date much in high school. However, I do believe that it was because I was the only Catholic boy in my class. Later, I was told by a classmate that all the classmates respected me.

Of course, when boys became 15 or 16, the older boys would give them beer. We wanted to drink it as we felt we were more grown up and accepted. I had an auto accident when I was 16 because of drinking beer and wine. Also, when I was 18, I was in a serious accident with somebody else driving my car. The car turned over about nine times, and I was thrown from the car. I was sore for a while but did not go to the doctor. I knew I had to get away from that lifestyle, so I joined the Navy at 18 years old and have been on my own ever since.

The Navy was a good growing up experience. I never regretted the four years spent in the Navy. Also, during my teen years, my mother worked as a registered nurse at the Easton Memorial Hospital and at the Milford Memorial Hospital. Even though I had a lot of unsupervised times in my teen years, I felt sorry for my mom for having to work so much. Whenever I saw the clothes pile up, I would heat the water and wash the clothes and do the ironing for my mom.

I also cooked meals frequently. I did not feel compelled to do these things. I just felt sorry for my mom. She was educated but never got very much out of life for what she put into life. I am sure she is rewarded in heaven for all her sacrifices. Life is quite painful for some, the ones who don't get to feel a taste of the fruit that they had planted a long time ago, I mean, I feel like she deserved more in life, and I hope she gets that in heaven.

My father was always available to help somebody in need. He would stop whatever job he was on to answer the fire alarm.

He just had a bad habit of drinking and gambling. I don't blame him for the way he behaved with us. Every family has its ups and downs, and mostly we are a product of our surroundings. Our situation wasn't a cool breeze. It required struggle and effort from everyone in the family.

Rosie's Death

Rosie and I visited the Charlotte/Clover area in July 2016 to visit the children and especially for her to spend time with our great granddaughter, Vesper. We had a good visit and then, after spending some time, we started back to Florida. When we got back home, I told Rosie that I did not think I wanted to make that long trip anymore that year. She didn't protest.

We were just sitting and watching TV a few nights later and something struck me that I should take Rosie back to Clover, South Carolina, to spend time with our new great-granddaughter.

I told her to pack a few things, and that we were going to visit my granddaughter, Kelly. It seemed like a premonition that I should take her to see Vesper. We went to Clover, and she spent most of the week holding Vesper in her arms.

On the way home, we were met with horrible weather. I could see heavy dark clouds in all directions ahead. So, I said a little prayer and asked God to protect us on the way back home. Soon after, I could see a split in the clouds and the road was clear. At least six or seven times during the trip, I had to make the same prayer, and the roads cleared ahead of us every single time.

I think God showed His love for us and for the love we had for Vesper, because He protected us all the way back to Ft. Myers. Rosie passed away three or four days after we got back home. This seemed like divine intervention, and I think He let her live for her to shower her love to Vesper before she was called home.

RECORD OF MEDICAL TREATMENT FOR ROSIE

Rosie contracted diarrhea in her system on, Saturday, March 16, 2013.

March 17: Diarrhea became more frequent.

March 18-20: Diarrhea continued to worsen, and I contacted Dr. Ken Smith, who is Rosie's family doctor. He suggested that we contact Dr. Mackler of Seaford, as he would be better qualified to get to the source quicker.

March 21: I contacted Dr. Mackler's office and was given an appointment for March 22 at 9:30 a.m.

March 21: Rosie continued to worsen and was a little incoherent, so I decided to call the ambulance for transfer to hospital. I advised Dr. Mackler's office of the decision and was told that if she was released from hospital to keep the appointment.

March 21: Rosie was transported to the emergency room of Nanticoke Memorial Hospital. Upon arrival around lunch time she was given a room in the emergency department. She was seen by a nurse and an IV was started. She was seen by a doctor, and it was determined that she had an intestinal virus (viral gastroenteritis). She was ready to be released and told to contact her family doctor for follow-up treatment. As she was preparing to leave the emergency room, she had to go to the bathroom. I advised the staff several times that Rosie was very weak. She went into the bathroom, and she fell as she was getting off the stool. At least four or five people responded immediately to assist in getting her off the floor. She was taken back to her room. As I was waiting for the release papers to arrive, Rosie removed the IV and a lot of blood began to leak. I immediately put a bandage over it and called for help. Before assistance came, she was moving the blanket back and forth several times. I asked her what she was doing, and she replied she was putting her shirt on. I told her I had just put her shirt on, and she continued to try to find the sleeve holes. I went out and found a nurse and told him I was really concerned about her being released because of her recent behavior about the IV and her shirt. He shined a light into her eyes and asked her name and her birth date. She responded correctly, and I was told that she was OK for release. They released her around 6:15 p.m. for a total stay of over six hours in the emergency room. No blood work was done and the only thing I recall being done was an IV. They gave her a prescription for Ondansetron 8 mg and Dicyclomine 10 mg which I filled, and she started taking. Up to that point, nothing had any effect on the frequency of diarrhea.

March 22: I took Rosie for an appointment with Dr. Mackler at 9:30 a.m. He saw her, and I advised him she was continuing to get worse. I told him of the prescriptions the hospital had ordered and he said there was nothing any better for her condition and that she should continue taking the prescriptions and should get better in a few days. I left his office and took her home. She continued to grow weaker and to have diarrhea more frequently.

March 23: On Saturday morning I called Dr. Mackler and told him she was continuing to decline and that I was going to call the ambulance again and take her to the emergency room. He said that he would stop by and see her. He did not come on Saturday. She stayed in the ER most of the day and it they admitted her. They did some blood work and a CAT scan of her abdominal area. I understood that she probably had either a blockage or an enlargement of the intestine that was not allowing food to be digested and that they would admit her.

She was admitted and assigned a doctor, a very knowledgeable young East Indian woman, who thoroughly explained

Rosie's condition and explained a course of action. She was concerned that Rosie's heart was not stable and said she wanted to stabilize the heart before doing much for the diarrhea. She also explained that several of Rosie's blood chemistries were not stable and that her electrolytes were low. Rosie had four IVs going at the same time. I was satisfied with the treatment that had been prescribed. The doctor came to the ER and advised me that she would be the one person responsible for my wife's care. I really appreciated her direct approach and willingness to explain the problem to us in layman's terms. The diarrhea was still really bad and continued to get worse. Rosie was becoming more incoherent by the hour.

March 24: Rosie was in a private room and was not acting normally. She removed her IV several times. I saw Rosie around 12 noon and was advised to not go in, as the room was in a terrible state with fecal matter all over. My daughter Dorothy looked in and stated that it was awful, and that Rosie was in the bathroom. I talked with the nurse, Kim, and was told that housekeeping had been called and that we should go get lunch and that they would clean the room while we were gone. We went to the hospital lunchroom and when we returned, the room was clean. I told Kim that it would be unacceptable for my wife to be exposed to these conditions in the future and that I wanted her to have adult panties. Kim stated she did not have any, but would find some. She came back with adult diapers. I told Kim that I would go to Walmart and get some adult panties for Rosie. I bought some adult panties, and she was able to use them to avoid spilling fecal matter all over the room.

I repeatedly told the staff that Rosie had no control over her bowel movements and that she could not make it to a potty or the bathroom in time. I had been scrubbing the floors at home every couple of hours, both day and night, for the last several days.

Dr. Mackler came in and as we talked, he advised me that I was confused about the condition of my wife. I told him that the previous doctor had advised us that the heart was the major concern and that the diarrhea would be taken care of after the heart was stabilized. He told me that the two things were totally separate and not related to each other. He said that he had been in constant consultation for the entire day around my wife's condition and that she was being treated for the diarrhea as a separate issue not associated with the heart problem.

We requested that Dr. Mackler be removed from Rosie's care as it was difficult to understand what he was adding to her medical recovery. He did not offer any plan on what he was considering if he remained closely associated with her condition.

Rosie continued to have less control of her state of mind. She asked us if we saw the beautiful hummingbirds in the IV. As the staff and Dorothy were leaving the room, Rosie started to get out of bed and pulled the IV cord to the fully extended position. I stopped her and asked her what she was doing, and she said that she was going to go down with them. She did not recognize that she was hooked up to an IV, and that she was confined to the bed.

She had a CAT scan of her head to determine if maybe she had had a stroke. I was told that the results of the scan were negative and that she has not had a stroke. Kim, the nurse, went off duty at 7 p.m. and Rachel came on. Rachel was training someone, but she was very approachable and provided me with information at each request. We made the decision that Rosie should have continuous assistance, so somebody was assigned to stay with her that night. Rosie had become more agitated as she was transferred to a room with a roommate. I was told that she was transferred because the other person in the room also needed constant support during the night. Rosie was in a higher state of aggravation as I left her room around 9:30 that night. My daughter Dorothy spent the night with her.

March 26: Rosie was released and came home at 5:40 p.m. I got an appointment for the next day and filled three prescriptions ordered by the hospital doctor.

March 27: I took Rosie to see Dr. Smith at 11 a.m. She was still weak and got up four times during the night to use the bathroom. Dr. Smith advised us to follow release orders from hospital. He stated that she still was dehydrated as he examined her tongue. The visiting nurse from Christiana Health Care visited and did an evaluation. She said she would return on Friday and said she would send someone to help Rosie take a bath.

I had an appointment with Dr. Simon for the next Monday at 9:30 a.m. to examine Rosie's heart. I also had an appointment in Cape Coral with Dr. Kini, a gastroenterologist, for an office visit and to schedule a colonoscopy for April 24 at 9:30. I filled four more prescriptions written by the visiting nurse. I called Dr. Gardner's office (our orthopedic doctor in Florida) and asked him to recommend a cardiologist. I tried to call Dr. Joseph Aloise, our family doctor in Ft. Myers, but could not reach him.

March 28: we made an appointment with Dr. Scala of Cape Coral (our Florida heart doctor) for April 29 at 2 p.m.

March 29: The visiting nurse indicated Rosie was doing well. She advised Rosie to stop taking Triamterene as some other medicine was taking its place. She said she would visit again on Tuesday of the next week. We had not yet had an aide visit. Holly, the aide, will try to make that visit happen. Holly said that we would get a call concerning the time of the visit.

Dr. Robert J Davis, Rosie's breast cancer plastic surgeon, had recommended we see Dr. Lorraine M Golosow. I would call for an appointment. I made contact with Dr. Golosow's office, and they said they would get the records from Dr. Davis's office. The appointment was set for May 1 at 1:15 p.m.

April 1: We visited Dr. Simon at 9:30 in the morning. He performed a complete physical, and also did an EKG and ordered additional blood work. The EKG showed a slight additional beat, but the rhythm was good. He ordered Xarelto as a blood thinner and said to take one-half hour prior to the evening meal. He also told me to keep a close observation for blood. He recommended the following medication changes: 1- discontinue taking aspirin; 2- cut the Clonidine tablet in half and take it two times a day since it only has an eight-hour life; 3- cut metoprolol tartrate tablet in half and take twice daily. Dr. Simon commented that Rosie's medications were very confusing and that we should have the visiting nurse review what she was taking and determine the proper time to take it.

April 2: Rosie was up at 8:00 with eight hours of sleep. Only up one time during the night for the bathroom. A visiting nurse, Kimberly Banks, came at 9:30. She discussed medications and advised that the system we use for what and when to take the medications was a good one. I asked about using the sheet that came with the visiting nurse package. She said that they normally do that with someone that is not organized and does not understand when to take medications. She took blood pressure, and it was 94 over 66. She advised that Dr. Simon had changed her medication and that should allow blood pressure to go down. She checked her heart and said it was normal. She asked if Rosie had any pain and Rosie told her she had none. She asked about bowel movements and Rosie told her it was normal. She asked if we had any other questions or concerns, and we had none. She said an aide had been ordered and should come soon. She told us a physical therapist was scheduled for a visit at 3:30. I bought a cane for Rosie that night from Walmart.

The therapist, Nicki, came at 5:30 and stayed about an hour. She checked Rosie's mobility for arms and legs and checked the bathroom and bed and had Rosie get on and off. Nicki stated that Rosie was not immobile enough to justify things to help her walk or get in and out of bed or use the hopper. She told Rosie to go to the emergency room immediately if she fell. She also recommended that Rosie use a cane for stability while walking. Nicki left and said she would return on Thursday.

April 13: We had an auction at the Bridgeville address, and we left for Florida at 4:00 p.m. We stopped at Waldorf, Maryland, for the night as Rosie was in severe pain. We left the hotel at 8:00 a.m. and as I was bringing the car to pick up Rosie at the front door. She fell onto the sidewalk but wasn't hurt. She could not get up, as she was very weak. I picked her up, and we started the drive to South Carolina.

We continued to Clover, South Carolina, and spent the night at our granddaughter's house, but Rosie continued to be in severe pain.

April 14: We left Clover at 8 a.m. and planned to drive to Brunswick, Georgia, for the night. Rosie was in such pain that we decided to drive all the way to Ft. Myers. We arrived there around 7 p.m. and got a carryout pizza for dinner. Rosie was unable to walk.

April 15: I called the ambulance and had Rosie taken to Cape Coral Hospital. They did tests in the emergency room for most of the day, including several blood tests. They decided to hold her in the outpatient clinic for the night, and they gave her morphine for the pain, and she slept well for the night.

April 16 and 17: Rosie was examined, and they decided the problem was gout. She had not taken her gout medicine since being told by the Seaford hospital to stop taking it. Rosie was seen by a physical therapist and given instructions to do six exercises.

April 18: Rosie was doing much better with very little pain. She could now walk with no support and the doctor said she could be released and that we should make an appointment with our family doctor for follow-up.

April 19: Visited Dr. Aloise, Rosie's family doctor, and he examined her. He stated she should begin taking the gout medicine again and to make a follow-up appointment for three months.

April 20 and 21: Rosie continued to feel better and was walking without a cane.

April 24: Rosie visited Dr. Kini, the gastroenterologist, and he advised she did not need a colonoscopy and that she should follow a good diet. Another visit was scheduled for May 15.

April 29: Visited Dr. Scala, the heart specialist in Florida. He examined Rosie and requested a heart stress test. He could not find any atrial fibrillation (AFib) at this time. He advised her to continue with Xarelto as a blood thinner to prevent a stroke and said she might have to stay on it for a long time.

May 1: Dr. Scala performed a heart stress on Rosie. The test was done over a four-hour period. She was scheduled to go back in two weeks for the results.

That same day, Rosie visited Dr. Lorraine Golosow, the breast cancer plastic surgeon in Florida. She did an examination of Rosie's breast and said that the lumps she felt were the scar tissue associated with the implants and that she had no concern that it might be cancer. She also stated that what Dr. Davis was doing in Salisbury was also done by three doctors in Ft. Myers. She advised us to make appointments with a cancer doctor and a cancer surgeon, as well as for an echocardiogram.

May 15: Visited Dr. Kini. Rosie had no gastrointestinal problems, and he said her recent problem at Seaford was most likely a parasite in food. He told her to see her family doctor for ongoing pain and to come back as needed.

May 16: Visited Dr. Aloise for pain. He examined her legs and said that the problem might be associated with the blood arteries and that an ultrasound test should be done. He advised that Dr. Scala had the equipment in his office, and we could get it done on our visit. He also gave us some samples of Xarelto as our prescription program had been canceled. Rosie only has to go back as required. He provided a prescription for a combination of acetaminophen and codeine for pain. He also provided a prescription for Daypro 600 mg but asked us to clear it with Dr. Scala first.

May 16: Visited Dr. Scala. He advised that the results of the heart stress test indicated she had no major problems with her heart. However, since she had three out of five indicators for stoke probability, she should stay on Xarelto for the undetermined future. The pain in her legs was probably coming from a problem in the knee. He suggested going to a knee specialist and set another appointment for November 2013. He also advised us to not fill the prescription for Daypro as it could cause bleeding.

June/July: Rose seemed to be holding on and maybe getting a little better. The main earlier problem was probably from contaminated food received in Seaford just prior to leaving for Florida. I noticed her dog seemed to pay closer attention to her in late July. Normally, he would just stay on the floor close to her. Lately he got closer to her and seemed to understand that she was not well.

August 2, 2014: Rosie passed away at 8:30 p.m. It was a quick passing as she only had to suffer for about 30 minutes while I took her to the emergency room.

It is hard losing a person who shared half their life with you. She was just amazing and when she left, I could feel a hollow space in my chest, and I had to carry it everywhere with me. I documented my behavior and progress as her death made me a vessel empty of liquid, and it took me some time to gain back the part of me I had lost with her departure.

On August 1 around 10:30 p.m., Rosie told me she was having pain in the face and neck area and had to get to the hospital. When she got to the ER, she told us that the pain was a nine on a scale of ten, so the doctor ordered morphine for her.

Over the next three hours, they performed several tests and her heart, blood pressure, and blood sugar were all within limits. The doctor advised that he was going to admit Rosie for further tests and observation. She asked me to go home around 2:30 a.m. as she felt fine. I went home and got three hours of sleep and went to work at the Pro-Shop at Sabal Springs.

The hospital called me around 10 a.m. and told me they were going to transfer Rosie to another hospital for surgery. I left immediately after the call and proceeded to Health Park Hospital.

When I got there, they said they had to begin the surgery before my arrival. Rosie underwent open-heart surgery for about eight hours while I waited in the open hallway. The staff looked after me very well. The doctor allowed our priest, Father Tom, to enter the operating room and give Rosie the last rites.

Around 9:00 p.m., the heart surgeon told me that he did everything he could but that he could not save her. She had an aortic dissection on the top side of the heart. Everything happened so fast that it did not seem real. I could feel myself fading into nothingness as if I was the one who had left this world, not her.

I had Rosie transferred to Greensboro, Maryland, for funeral arrangements. Her funeral was a catholic mass and burial in Catholic cemetery on Denton highway in Greensboro.

Her brother, Carl, sponsored a dinner for everyone. He was very kind and provided housing for me during the funeral.

The first three weeks after her passing were very hard to take in what happened. I had a good support network in the church and constant contact with Dorothy and Kelly. Butch and Eddie also kept in close contact with me. I heard from Karen and Lisa routinely, but Sharon did not contact me.

I felt like I was getting better, but I took everything one day at a time. I was not sure of my immediate plans to relocate and figured it would probably take at least a year to decide if I wanted to move in with one of the children.

September 21, 2014: Things got a little better each day. I slept well from around 11 p.m. until 6 and sometimes 7 a.m. I drove to the Clover/Charlotte area in early September and spent a week with my children. I was able to see Luke in a football game. He was happy going to a Catholic School in the seventh grade. Little Vesper seemed to take to me well as she did with Rosie. I worked at the Pro-shop as needed. The manager interviewed a new pro, but I continued to help as needed, but I decided I did not want to be on a regular schedule of working.

November 5, 2014: The girls decided to have a get-together for Thanksgiving at Lisa's house, with everyone except Sharon attending. This was nice, and Rosie would have been so happy. I drove to Brunswick on the 5th and drove the rest of the way on the 6th. It was not as stressful to divide the trip into two days as it was on a one-day trip. I spent a lot of time with Dorothy, Kelly, and their families.

On November 7, 8, and 9: I took Mitch, Gabe, and Luke to Charleston to watch Mitch play lacrosse for a traveling lacrosse team. Mitch was an amazing player. We had a great time with the boys, getting plenty to eat and joking and cutting up at nighttime.

It was a tiring weekend, but I enjoyed spending time with the boys. I planned to go spend the evening and night with Luke later that week. I planned to go with Mark and Luke for a hunting trip during the Thanksgiving holiday. I was getting a little more used to being without Rosie, but I prayed for her each day and still try to attend mass daily. I thought about re-locating to Charlotte so that I could spend more time with my family. Loneliness can overwhelm you, but being around loved ones is always a treat.

February 1, 2015: I had been staying inside nearly the whole time since Rosie died. I finally decided that I would start living again. I called the Realtor and put the house up for sale. I had been very protective of myself and had allowed nobody to get close to me, but I decided to leave Florida, as it was not the same without Rosie. I did not know what my next move would be, whether I would settle in an apartment or maybe a condo.

My Realtor told me she thought my home would sell quick-ly. Within one week, she came back with four signed contracts. Three were for cash. I accepted the one that was for $500.00 more than the asking price.

Karen, Mark, and Lisa came to Florida and helped me pack. I rented a U-Haul truck and had it packed tight. Mark drove the U-Haul. When I say drove, I mean we had to drive 80 to 85 mph to keep up with him sometimes. I moved all my things into my place in Clover. I had a small bedroom downstairs and used the front room for my office and storage of boxes. It worked for a while, but I would make some changes in the future. I felt like I needed to be alone and at least not that close to family members. It was great spending time with Kelly and her two children, and Vesper allowed me to hold her just about any time and she gave me kisses.

April 2015: My realtor gave me a list of some things that need to be done before listing my home in Clover, South Carolina. I replaced the damaged siding that was hit by the weed whacker. I also needed to repaint several rooms. Dorothy repainted some rooms dark green and some ruby colors. These were colors she liked, but the realtor stated the colors should be neutral to support the sale.

I started painting right away. I thought I might need to replace the countertops, as they had some cut spots on them. I didn't mind spending money on repairs, since a house in the best condition usually brings the most money at sale.

I relaxed and went to an Elton John concert in Greenville with Dorothy and really enjoyed the show.

May: Dorothy graduated from college with her master's degree in social services during the first week of May. She was now getting the papers together for the state exam to get her certificate. She had applied for several jobs in the 100-mile range of Charlotte.

Mitch had been accepted to Wesley College in Dover, Delaware, with a scholarship to play lacrosse. He was selected as the most valuable defensive player on the varsity lacrosse team at Clover High, and Gabe had started playing lacrosse at Clover that year.

Getting Out

In May 2015, I started taking some ladies out for lunch and getting to know more about them. I did not make it a secret that my intentions were to find that special person who I want to spend the rest of my life with.

I joined Catholic Mates, a dating service for Catholics. You must fill out many questions to develop a profile. They send you profiles of people that have similar interests. I have met many ladies. However, I had pretty much narrowed it down to four that I had some interest in, as they were close to where I lived. None of the acquaintances had been romantic.

Gerri is 63 years old and had shown a significant interest in me; she seemed like a nice person. I defined under 70 years as an age limit for considering a relationship.

May 17, 2015: It had been several weeks since I had written anything down. I continued to pray for Rosie's soul to be beside God in His heavenly court. I prayed for her every night and each time that I attended Mass. I did not know if I would ever get over her, but I made the decision that I wanted to share my life with another human being that is not a family member.

No matter how much I loved and love Rosie, the fact is that I will never see her again on this earth. I think it is God's will that we share our life and love for Him with other people. Family is not the same as having a special mate to share all of your love with and sharing moments that are special to a married couple, but not necessarily special to family and friends. We all need a partner, no matter how great a family is. I felt I needed one, too.

I have enjoyed going to most of Mitch's and Gabe's lacrosse games whenever I saw them. I attended Luke's football games and went to most of his baseball games. He was on a summer traveling team, and I planned to continue supporting him.

Since her passing, I had been mourning and missing Rosie. I do not enjoy living alone. I needed to have a significant other with whom I could share my life and love.

When I joined the Catholic Mates group, I was very truthful about my profile, stating that I was 76 years old and in excellent health. I had shared information with probably 30 ladies and taken six or seven out to lunch. It was easier to manage four that I was really interested in and had more than one date with.

It was getting a little old trying to keep all the names straight and finding excuses because I could not see somebody on a certain day. I finally agreed to see only one lady for the next few months, intending to marry her if we continued to get along well.

She was 63 years old. There were several others in their 60s that had a keen interest in me. Anyway, I hoped to marry Gerri sometime after Christmas. I met some of her family and they indicated they approved of me.

Lisa and Luke had also met her and gave their support. I decided to tell Dorothy soon and felt she would probably accept it, but not be overly supportive.

I had also seen Marylyn several times. She was thin and cute with blond hair and had a place on the water and a really cute red Mercedes Benz convertible. We got along well, but I don't think we were made for each other. She is Catholic and goes to church regularly, but I noticed she was forgetful. She also seemed to get overly excited about things. She told me she was not honest with me about her age. She said that she was 63, but she was really 68 years old. Anyway, I wrote her a Dear John letter and told her I would not see her again.

July 19, 2015: We held a Gardner family reunion in Maryland at the Tuckahoe State Park in Centerville. It was nice, but very hot. Nearly all my family members were present except my brother's family. Only Dickie and Anna Mae were there. We had some very good group pictures, and Karen and Frank provided sleeping accommodations for me. They also supplied plenty of crabs for two good crab parties. I provided beer and ice. Karen also provided food for all the family members who stayed at her house for several nights. Mark and Lisa invited me to ride along to the family get-to-gather, and I accepted. It was a pleasant trip with them doing all the driving.

July 21, 2015: I discontinued seeing the lady I mentioned earlier. I sent Gerri an email over the weekend telling her I did not feel right about our relationship and that I did not want to see her anymore in a romantic status and I told her we were okay. She wanted me to go with her to two weddings. I had said that I would go, but then had second thoughts, so I sent her the email letting her know I would not attend the weddings.

She was a nice lady, but she was a little too forward for me. We progressed too far too fast. She had no opinion about anything. She just told me that the only thing she wanted to do was to always please me. I decided she was not the one for me to marry. I had a very busy time dating.

Karen told me she did not know how I kept it all straight. I was dating three ladies at the same time, and sometimes I would have to leave one to get back in town soon enough to meet the next one.

I contacted Miriam from Burlington, whom I had taken out one time to the Childress winery. She was happy to hear from me and had told me earlier that she would be available if I broke up with Gerri.

She was a very nice lady, very cute, and 68 years of age. She is a devout Catholic and has her own financial resources. She told me I am the only person who she has dated since her husband died five years ago. I have really good feelings for her. We both want to find the special person to spend the rest of our life with.

July 21, 2015: I still think about Rosie a lot and prayed every night for her soul to be resting in peace in heaven. She had been gone a year. I will continue to miss her, but I did not want to spend the rest of my life living alone.

I tell any lady that I take out on the first date that I am looking for a long-term relationship that leads to marriage. Most of the ladies are also looking for someone to share their life with.

Miriam - My New Mate

In July 2015, I spent time with Miriam. We had a good day and got to know each other much better. First, we went to Zimmerman's Vineyard close to Asheboro, North Carolina, where we had a wine tasting and then we went to the Asheboro Zoo.

We had lunch at the Zoo and walked through many of the areas and got back to the Vineyard around 4 p.m. for a show that was performed every second Saturday of the month.

The show did not start until 5:30, so we sat under the trees and enjoyed a bottle of wine. Since she liked the white Merlot, we got a bottle and talked until the show started.

The wine ran out around 5:30, and we decided to get another. We enjoyed each other's company and the music and friends until 9:00. I had little or no effects from the wine, so I drove the two hours back to Charlotte.

We felt we had a lot in common and we got along just fine. She invited me to meet her daughter in Norfolk and spend Thanksgiving with them.

We began discussing the possibility of getting married after getting to know each other better. She had her own home in Burlington, North Carolina, and said that she would like to live in that area if possible. I told her I would have no problem with that area if we decided we were for each other.

We both agreed that we needed to spend more time together before we started making marriage plans. We were both looking for that special person to spend the rest of our life with, and neither of us were looking for a short-term relationship.

Miriam

August 14: Dorothy, Kelly, and their families were planning a trip to Ocean City for one week's vacation. I gave Dorothy and their family a week's paid vacation to just get away and relax.

September 1: Miriam and I were getting along very well. I planned to visit her again late in the week, leaving on Thursday and probably coming back on Sunday. We both agreed that I would stay until Sunday.

We began to think that we were compatible, and I believed she was the one that I wanted to spend the rest of my life with. Karen and Lisa were both quite supportive. However, Dorothy did not want to discuss the situation or even hear about it. Miriam and I talked in detail about the possibility of getting married. We discussed with one another that we will not have a sexual relationship until our wedding night. It is very lonely living alone. God gives us a chance to gain new experiences and meet new people in life. I believed that if I found someone worth sharing my life with, I had the right to witness that happiness.

I became involved with the church and went to Mass regularly. I joined the K.O.C., the Right To Life Group, and the E.M. I attended Mass with Miriam at her church and told her that at the Sign of Peace, I would shake her hand rather than kiss her because the people in the church would notice me with her. We sat in the second row from the front. When the Sign of Peace came, she grabbed my head and gave me a kiss in front of the entire church. It really felt good that she was so comfortable with me and didn't care about the peeping eyes.

August 14, 2015: I put my Clover, South Carolina, house on the market in late July and informed Dorothy that I was going to sell the house and that I would appreciate her allowing realtors to show it. I told her I would provide housing for her and Gabe if the house sold. I had the house on the market for a week and got a show. I lowered the asking price by $10,000 and offered the selling realtor a $1000 bonus for selling the house. It got sold in two days for the full price with some conditions. I told Dorothy again that I would provide housing for her and Gabe if she did not find employment by the time the house was to settle. Kelly later told me that Dorothy and Gabe were moving in with her.

After selling the Clover house, I had more time to concentrate on finding the proper lady. After many lunch dates and movie dates, I decided Miriam was the one for me. I also had strong feelings for two other ladies, but let them know I would not see them anymore.

I was thrilled being with Miriam and planned to marry her. I

The author, Jim Gardner, and Miriam

gave her an engagement ring, and we decided to marry after the first year. Karen and Lisa were supportive. However, I tried to talk to Dorothy about my relationship with Miriam a couple of times and she told me she did not want to hear anything about it. I think Dorothy just loved me and would rather not share me with anybody.

I know that when I married Miriam, Dorothy would have to accept her, or I could not be as supportive of Dorothy. I planned to visit Miriam on her birthday, and we would travel to Gainesville, Virginia, so that I could meet her daughter. We planned a trip to Little Rock, Arkansas, during the Christmas holidays to visit her son Walker. Miriam told me that I could move in with her whenever I wanted to. She had a nice three-bedroom home with two bathrooms. We were getting along very well.

September: We made the trip to meet Miriam's son, Walker. It was a pleasant trip, and we all got along well. It was a two-day trip, as we did not want to drive long hours. We visited friends of Miriam's in Mississippi on the way back.

October: We continued to see each other nearly every weekend. Usually, we would just see a movie or attend a playhouse show. We would always attend mass together on Sunday morning.

November: I still stayed in my apartment in Clover and stayed close to Lisa, Dorothy, and Kelly.

I would normally have dinner with Lisa once a week and help with some maintenance when needed.

December: Miriam and I were both satisfied with getting married now that we had spent so much time together. We had a great Christmas with families at various locations. My lease on my apartment expired in February, so Miriam asked if I wanted to move in with her in Burlington, North Carolina. It sounded like the right thing to do.

January 27, 2016: I moved in with Miriam on January 9. I had been working for the past three weeks trying to combine two houses into one. Finally, I could get two cars into her garage. I had a storage unit with a lot of stuff in it. We had a hot tub installed just outside of the deck. It was a nice one with ten jets, and we used it nearly every night. I purchased a new 2016 KIA Sorrento in November.

Miriam was nice and considerate of me. She fixed good meals every day, however, we ate out a couple of times a week with folks from church. I joined both the third- and fourth-degree Knights of Columbus in Burlington.

We went to church every week together, and I was happy and content with things at that point, but I still prayed for the soul of Rosie every day.

It was an adjustment to start living with another mate. However, I accepted I would never see Rosie again. So, I believed God wanted us to be happy and share our love with each other.

February 10, 2016: Things were going well with Miriam, and I was happy living with her. She continued to be kind, considerate, and loving toward me. We got along well and did not seem to have any issues. She always went out of her way to satisfy me and offered to do things for me.

I had been very busy for the past weeks arranging her home and storing things. She had an oversize two-car garage that was so jammed packed that you could not walk in it.

I had all the things stored and labeled and we could finally park two cars in the garage with plenty of room. I knew it upset her a little that I was pushing her to get things organized, but I told her I had to have things in an orderly fashion. I am a well-organized person. It is a carryover from my working years. I would not have survived if I was not well organized.

Two cats and a dog were sleeping in the bedroom. I convinced her we do not need any animals sleeping in the bedroom. The carpet was horrible because of the animals, and I replaced the carpet with hardwood and helped her clean up all the extra stuff from the rest of the rooms in the house.

We went to church every week and ate out with church friends two or three times a week. I was becoming active in the Knights of Columbus and went to all meetings. I volunteered to maintain the flower arrangement at a special shrine at the church.

The weather was cold. This was the first time in ten years that I had been in the north during the winter months. I was tolerating the weather very well and really did not mind it too much. We shared our monthly income, and it appeared we had a cash flow of around $100,000 per year. So, it seemed like we could live well for the rest of our lives. This did not count our individual investment income. She told me she had filed income taxes the past year on $100,000. We planned to travel a lot. I told her I could provide $10,000 for travel each year for as long as we lived.

March 12: Mariam & I married on March 12, 2016. It was a traditional Catholic Church wedding. I felt good and still had a lot of energy at 77 years old. It was a really nice church wedding. Father Jerry of Elon College married us. He is a good friend of Miriam's. We had a nice reception at our home, and we had about 80 attendants. It went well and everybody seemed to have a good time. We served wine and beer but decided not to provide any whiskey.

We had plenty of food and told lots of good stories to the crowd for entertainment's sake. I was happy my friends Chuck Steward of Richmond, Joe Little, and Carl Zlock came. They have all been close friends of mine for many years. We left for Charlotte the next day to fly to Cancun for a week-long vacation.

May 24, 2016: Miriam and I had been married for two months now and were still getting along very well. We had a meeting a couple of weeks ago to make sure that neither of us had any issues that we needed to discuss. We both had a couple of things to sort out, things that the other one did that were creating issues for the other person. We discussed and committed that we would try to avoid the issues in the future. If one of us was irritated by something the other was doing, we would call a meeting and discuss the issue. We both believe that communication is the first and most significant step in marriage.

We were traveling a lot and didn't get a chance to visit my family very much after our trip to Alaska. We took a Viking cruise from Washington to Alaska. It was a great trip, and we really enjoyed seeing the glaciers. We stopped at a small village, and they had salmon prepared for us. It was the best salmon you could ever image. The trip was an all-inclusive thing, with all the food and drinks provided at no extra fee. Miriam was still very considerate of me and did many nice things for me daily. I fixed many things in her house. She talked about selling it in a few years. We planned a trip to Florida to look for a winter home there.

June 16, 2016: I had the opportunity to drive an official NA-SCAR Cup car around the Charlotte speedway. It was #77. It was a very hot day, and I was suited up for at least two hours before I got into the car.

Once I managed to get in through the door window, it was tight inside. I slipped the steering wheel on and waited for my command to start.

I had trouble with the clutch and getting the car to start. The second time I got it going and shifted gears as I instructed by my spotter, shifting at 3000 rpm. I had an eight-minute ride with no pace car or restrictions.

My helmet was way too big and slid down over my eyes. I had to hold it up with my left hand and drive with my right hand. After a couple of laps, I got the feel of the car and found out that I really had to slow down for only one corner. I was told to hold it at 4000 rpm all the way around. After a few laps, I let it go some more. Going into the first turn, I held it to the floor and continued to hold it down on the backstretch. The engine started missing as I hit 5500 rpm. I could get over 155 mph out of it, but the spotter told me to slow down, and then told me to hit my brakes.

As I hit my brakes, I noticed I was coming up behind another driver too fast. I slowed it down in plenty of time, and then was told to come off the track as my time was up. It was really a lot of fun, considering I was turning 78 years old soon.

July 3, 2016: I was very satisfied with my life. We went to church nearly every week, and I met many people at Blessed Sacrament Catholic Church in Burlington, North Carolina.

We normally ate out three times a week with three different groups of friends, made up of either K.O.C. members or the wives of deceased members. I attended both third and fourth degree K.O.C. meetings each month and helped with several activities. Miriam and I maintain the flowers at the K.O.C. memorial at the church. I pick up trash from the roadside with other knights. Also, I enjoy going to the V.A. hospital in Durham to conduct bingo games for the patients.

I contributed $900.00 monthly to support the household expenses at Miriam's home. That amount included half the property taxes and half the home insurance. We attended some of Luke's baseball games and we visited Lisa, Dorothy, and family, along with Kelly's family, in Charlotte. We decided we would probably not purchase a home in Florida.

The only real issue I had with life was my weight. I had tried several things and couldn't seem to lose weight. I gained about 15 pounds since Rosie died and couldn't seem to get it off. We planned to join a gym and my doctor said he would help me with a program on my next visit. I started a low carb and no sugar eating plan and lost about 15 pounds in the first two weeks. I could eat just about anything that did not contain carbs.

Miriam loved to travel and go out and talk with friends. We rented a townhouse in Florida for the month of February 2017.

September 8, 2016: Miriam and I returned from a seven-day cruise to Alaska. It was a good trip. We visited several cities on the coast, visited Glacier Bay, and saw the glaciers. We enjoyed dinner in an outside setting with fresh salmon. The ship carried around 3500 passengers and the food was good and nearly always available. We did not overeat and enjoyed several formal dinners. The weather was great, with the temperature ranging in the 60s during the day. We had wine at most meals but did not over-drink. It was good to be back home again.

September 17: Miriam's birthday was on September 16. I gave her a birthday party, with many of the K.O.C. members and their wives joining us. Her daughter and family attended the event, as did Dorothy and Gabe. We had plenty of food and drinks and a pit fire. Everyone had a good time and the younger folks stayed until late evening. I took quite a few pictures.

October 10: Miriam and I were getting along well. The only conflict we had was with her two cats. I had mentioned to her how much I dislike cats and am allergic to them. She agreed to have the 14-year-old cat put down because of its poor health.

I suggested she should find a home for the other cat as well, as we wanted to do a lot of traveling. We planned a trip to Florida for the entire month of February 2017. She also had a dog, but I told her I would not suggest getting rid of it until it was in poor health.

November-December 2016: We visited Lisa and Mark for Thanksgiving dinner. It was a pleasant visit with Dorothy and Lisa and Karen, all getting along just fine. Everybody brought their favorite dish, and I overate because of the great food. Mark and Luke went back to the farm for deer hunting. We had Christmas at our place in Burlington. I think we had 21 people for dinner and both Dorothy and family came and also Lisa and family. Karen was on a cruise, so she couldn't make it.

January 2017: Miriam and I had planned a cruise for ten days in the south Atlantic islands. We flew to Ft. Lauderdale to meet the ship. We were going with two other couples from church, and we had planned to stay for a month in south Florida but had to change our plans because we made an offer on a home in Sabal Springs, Ft. Myers, and it was accepted. We scheduled settlement for around the 12th of February. We were both looking forward to spending a lot of time in Florida during the winter months and decided to move to Florida full time in 2018.

February 2017: Miriam and I were doing great. We have had our fair share of unpleasant or unloving conversations, but despite that, she was very nice to me. She had gotten rid of one cat but was dragging her feet on the other one. I had said that I would support her keeping the dog, but the cat was not a thing that needed to be discussed any further. I was very firm that I did not plan on having a cat in the house in Florida. We purchased a very nice home in Sabal Springs, in the North Ft. Myers area. We were both looking forward to making the move. She planned to keep the home in Burlington for 2017 and then sell it in 2018. Life was good!

July 15, 2020: We moved into a nice home with a large backyard and large oak trees on Pinewood Drive in New Bern, North Carolina.

Some Final Thoughts

My story is composed of clusters of experiences which I share with you, my readers, to witness. With all the adventures and struggles I have highlighted, I hope some of you might feel inspired and motivated.

A wise man said, if you are born poor, it is not your fault, but if you die poor, it is. We have the key to our lives in our hands. We decide on the outline and how we want to shape it. Never feel intimidated by changes or unanticipated events. They always have a lesson to offer, a push that will take you forward in life. Be the change you want in life and see how the world around you ignites in a preferred color.

My Ancestors and Notes

Much of the following information comes from census data or regional newspaper records. I have left the spellings and abbreviations the way they appear in those source documents.

Some information was provided by Mary Margaret Revell, a Maryland historian from Queen Anne's County.

James Richard Gardner was my great-great-grandfather. He was born in 1793 on Kent Island, Maryland, and died in 1870. He was married to Henretta Gooden/Goodon. According to the 1820 census, James Richard Gardner was the father of Richard J Gardner and lived in District 3 of Queen Anne's County, Maryland. The census record him living with 5 slaves and 10 people. In 1840, he had 5 slaves with 14 people.

In 1812, the British came up the Chesapeake Bay to take America back. When they got to Kent Island, they rested for a while, stopping at my great-great-grandfather's farm. I am not sure how long they stayed. However, they did take two slaves with them to help guide them up the Chesapeake Bay. It is not known what ever became of these two slaves.

The father of James Richard Gardner was Robert Gardner, who died in 1828. In January 1827, records show that Robert Gardner sold to James Richard, 1 head of cattle, 5 horses, 1 oxcart, 40 hogs, 20 head of sheep, 1800 wt. of port, 1 table, 5 chairs, 1 secretary, 1 clock, 1 bureau, 1 doz. chairs, 4 beds, bedding, bedsheets, 2 looking glasses, 3 chests, 1 gun, pair of irons, fodder, 1 canoe, 3 axes, 4 hoes, 2 doz. Knifes, 4 tubs, 2 spades.

Robert Gardner owed a huge debt to John McMullen over

a piece of land on Eastern Island. It was sold at court to highest bidder to pay debts. Highest bidder was Frances Gardner for the sum of $635.41 ¾.

John Hopkins, assignee of John McMullan recovered $233.33 1/3 plus damages of plus $7.61 2/3 court cost.

Richard J. Gardner was my great-grandfather. He was born on 12 May 1849 and died 11 Feb 1937 in Greensboro, Md. at the home of his son William. He is buried in Greensboro cemetery next to his wife, Sara. He has a small stone at the foot on the larger stone marking Sarah/Catherine. She was born in 1855 and died in Oct 24, 1920. They were married in 1877 or 1879. On the death certificate, his father is listed as James Richard Gardner, born on Kent Island, Maryland. He was a farmer his entire life. His mother is listed as Gooden and was born on Kent Island, Maryland.

From the *Denton Journal* in February 1937: Mr. and Mrs. M. F. Kibler celebrated their 27th wedding anniversary last Saturday night. The evening was spent in playing cards. Those present included Mr. & Mrs. Henry Wood and his son Jackie; Mr. & Mrs. Charles Vogt and sons Robert & Charles; Mr. & Mrs. J. Richard Gardner & Jean; Mr. & Mrs. Wm.. Gardner & children Barbara & Billy; Mr. & Mrs. R. J. Gardner; and Mr. & Mrs. Wm. R. Gardner and children Margaret, Pauline, and Francis. Several others attended.

Denton Journal February 20, 1937: Mr. Richard J. Gardner, age 87, died at the home of his son Wm. R. Gardner near town last Thursday morning after a few days of illness. He was not confined to his bed and his death was a shock to his many relatives and friends. Surviving are the following children: William Gardner of Greensboro; Mrs. Harry Adams of Cordova; Mrs. William Raughly of Wyoming, Delaware; two half-sisters; ten grandchildren, and seven great-grandchildren.

Funeral services were held at the home of his son, William Gardner of near Greensboro. Interment was in Greensboro Cemetery.

In the 1880 census, Richard was listed as a guest in the house of his father-in-law (William McClements) along with his wife Catherine/Sarah and son William, age 2. Richard's daughter Minnie C. Adams was born in 1879 and died in 1930. Minnie lived in the town Chaple in Talbot County, Maryland at the time of death.

In the 1900 census: Richard J Gardner, age 51, is head of house living in Centerville, Queen Anne's County, Maryland. Other people in the house include William R. Gardner, age 22; Sarah C. Gardner, age 50; and Etta, age 8. Rented farm.

1910 census: Richard lived in Representative District 6, Kent County, Delaware. His father and mother were born in Maryland. He was the head of the house. At age 32, William was not part of the household. Richard was age 61, Sarah was age 60, Minnie was age 29, and Etta was 20.

1930 census: Richard is age 81. Harry R Adams is age 61 and is head of the house. They lived at Chaple in Talbot County, Maryland. Minnie is age 51 and wife of Harry R. Adams and daughter of Richard. Mary C Adams is age 12 and Ross Adams is age 9. Richard J. is listed as widowed. His wife Catherine/Sarah died on 30 Oct. 1920. In 1930, Richard lived with his daughter Minnie on Matthews on Loveston Road, Chaple, Talbot County, Maryland.

R. J, Gardner Will: R.J. Gardner's wife (Catherine/Sarah) passed away in 1920. He might have remarried as he is listed as attending an affair with his wife.

Court record 1868: Richard Gardner 1868 wife Elizabeth (was he married twice or was there two Richard Gardners?) All Real Estate, personal effects to her son Richard J Gardner. To him all tract on east of public road running from Shark Tocon to Carson's Island called "Known as Cooper Hill" in fee simple also one negro woman Caroline.

Son Robert N Gardner on east side of Public road running from Shark Tocon to parsons Island is known as Cooper Hill in fee simple plus one negro boy Aldey & one negro woman Nancey.

Sons Herman & Samuel my homestead was known as Barns Sable Hill to be in simple fee. Hirman one negro woman Adalene.

Boy Joseph, his duck gun & ball rifle, and one bay mare flower. Samuel gets negro girl Hariett & boy Isaac. Sarah Elizabeth G. daughter of Robert N. – negro girl Tilly, Emily G. Daughter of David G. one negro girl Elen. Mary Rebecca G. Daughter of Robert N. G. 1 negro girl Haonor.

Robert's will: 1 sorrel horse & carriage, 1 negro boy, 1 n. g., 1 n woman Maria. Son Richard gets part of 3 tracts of land where he now lives at Coneyh Hall Barns Suble Hill and Gardner's Hardship. Daughter Ann Tolson, 1 negro boy Benjamin. Daughter Eliz Williams, 1 Negro woman Pat. 1 negro m Mint. Son Robert, negro man John & n w. temp. Daughter Martha Gardner, 1 n w Hannab, 1 negro w Poll. Son William, 1 negro boy Charles, 1 Negro child Harriet. My negro woman Sarah shall be free at my death. Son John, tract of land in Kent Co on Eastern Neck Island Chester Point, containing 300 acres land & 1 negro boy.

Catherine was my Great Grandmother: Born 2 July 1849 in Maryland. Died 30 October 1920 in Willow Grove, Delaware.

When Catherine (Sarah) McClements was born on July 2,

1849, her father, William, was 34 and her mother, Allminta was 29. She married Richard J. Gardner in 1877. They had four children in 13 years. She died on October 30, 1920, in Willow Grove, Delaware, at the age of 73, and is buried in the Greensboro, Maryland Cemetery. father was Wm. A McClemments, born 1815, and her mother was Allimite, born in 1820. Information from death certificate as provided by William Gardner, Goldsboro, Maryland 10/26/1920.

From *Denton Journal* Oct, 39, 1920: Mrs Sarah Catherine Gardner, age 73 years, died at her home near Willow Grove, De. on Saturday night last. The funeral was held at the late home of the deceased, Rev. Edwin Gardner, of Maryland officiating. Interment was made in Greensboro cemetery. William R. Gardner, Mrs. Harry Adams, and Mrs. William Raughley are children of the deceased. Wm. R. Gardner provided information for the death certificate.

• Note: no mention of the husband in the death certificate or Denton Journal. (Where they separated or divorced?)

Children: William R. Gardner (1878-1950) and Catherine (Minnie) Gardner (1880-1930), Etta W Gardner (died 1882), and Henrietta Elizabeth Gardner (1891-1984). Brother Robert was born in 1860. Catherine lived on Kent Island in 1880 at her father's home. On her death certificate, her father was listed as Wm. A McClements and her mother as Francis (Allimite) Hopkins.

William R. Gardner (My Grandfather): Born April 20, 1878, on Kent Island, Queen Anne's County, Maryland. Died 1950 in Greensboro, Maryland.

2 Jan 1909 - William R Gardner proceeds Mr. T. H. Robinson on Dr. M R Stephens Farm in Delaware.

From the *Denton Journal* January 2, 1909: Burrisville, Maryland. The changes to residence in this vicinity are more numerous than for years. Mr. Earnest Raughley who purchased a farm near Dover, has moved there. Mr. Wm. M Cheesum will occupy the farm vacated by Mr. Raughley. Mr. T. Wilton Porter will succeed Mr. Mr. Cheesum. Mr. W.T. Robinson purchased the C.A. Smith farm near Brownsville, Delaware, and has moved there with his family. Mr. Carroll Thawley of Delaware will occupy the Stephens homestead vacated by Mr. Robinson. Mr. Thomas II Robinson is Mr. Thawley's successor in Delaware. Mr. William Gardner of near Greensboro succeeds Mr. T II Robinson on the Dr. M. H. Stephens farm.

1910 census: Wm.. R. Gardner lived in Bursville/Denton, Md. Richard was age 0-1. Lists a Rowland Draper living with my grandfather.

18 Jan 1917: Grandmother's brother Philip Kibler, age 33, died in Greensboro.

29 Sept 1917: (maybe not related) William R. Gardner sold 74 Acres in 2nd district to Edwin Stephens.

From Recorder of Deeds Office: Luaher M Dill and his wife Mary E Dill to William R. Gardner and his wife Mary A. Gardner. This indenture made this 22 day of January 1918, between the Dills of Greensboro and the Gardner's of Murderkill Next Hundred, Kent County, Delaware. For the sum of $4500, $2000 cash and $2500 is secured by purchase money mortgage.

All that certain farm situated in Morah Murderkill Hundred, Kent County, Delaware. East side of Public Road leading from the Baptist Church and Petersburg Road to the Willow Grove Nand Choptank Mill Road. Next to Marsh Ditch, adjoin land of J Herman Gooden, lands Walter Peedler, lands of Alexander Dill and lands of others containing 189 acres. The same farm or tract of land which descended to the said Luaher M Dill from his father William Dill Who died intestate.

The 1920 census states that William R. Gardner's wife, Mary Kibler, my grandmother, was born in 1885 and lived in Greensboro in 1900.

1920 census: John R. Gardner (my father) lived with his father in Kent County, Delaware. He was 10 years old. Wm. R. Gardner was age 46, Mary A. Gardner age 33, John R. age 10, William age 8, Sarah age 6, Margaret age 4, Catherine age 3, Anna Age 2.

1930 census: Adds Pauline, age 10, and Francis, age 5. John Richard was not living at home in 1930.

From *Denton Journal* 21 July 1923: Property transfers: All that piece or parcel of land lying and being in Caroline County, Md. Being a part of a tract of land known as Painters Point, or by whatever name or names the same may be known. Beginning for the outlines on the same northeast corner of a lot sold by Joseph W Connelly to Wm. Gardner on the west side of county road leading from Upper Hunting Creek to Union Grove Church then with said road the following course: N. 47 deg. and 20 min, East 82 perches then north 59 degrees and 15 minutes west 35 4-10 perches then S. 47 deg. and 30 min W 36 perches to an old division line. Then with the said line S45 deg. E. 204 perches to the lot of land sold by said Joseph W. Connelly to Wm. Gardner Then with said lot the two following Courses Containing Seven and a Forth Acres and 35 square perches of land more or less. The track is 3 ½ acres clear and in high state of cultivation. (The description on identifies a Wm. Gardner and not a Wm. R. Gardner so I do not know if this was my grandfather.)

From *Denton Journal* 9, July 1927: Miss Elaine Newlin, who spent two weeks at the home of Mr. & Mrs. Wm. R. Gardner, has returned home to near Landenberg, Pa.

27 Dec 1924: Mr. John Ferriss of Tuckahoe Neck recently killed four hogs that weighed 370, 420, 375, and 385 lbs. An interesting fact in connection with the slaughter of these porkers is the weight of the butchers themselves. Mr. Ferriss and his two neighbors, Messes William Satterfield and William R. Gardner and Mr. Ferriss tips the scales at 245, Mr. Satterfield at 300 and Mr. Gardner at 270 lbs.

From the *Denton Journal* 15 May 1926: Public Sale, As I am going to leave the state, I will sell at public sale where I now live on the Wm. Gardner farm near Gafey's Mill Pond.

In 1927, Wm. R Gardner sold many farm/household/garden items due to moving out of state. Farm near Gary Mill Pond. Denton.

1930 census: Granddaddy lived in Greensboro, District 6 Part of 2nd election district. He was 52. Married at age 28 (1906). He had a radio and owned his farm.

25 Aug 1934: Grandmother visited Dad & Mom in Danvers and Grandmother spent a month in Danvers.

9 Nov 1935: Grandmother, Margaret, Clifford Bramble of Portland spent a week with Dad & Mom in Danvers.

9 June 1950: Granddaddy's sister Minnie lived in the Easton area. At one time, he lived off Liford-Lyford Road off Easton Road.

24 October 1920: Sarah C. Gardner (my grandfather's mother) died in Willow Grove Delaware. Wm. Gardner signed the death certificate.

Denton Journal 2 May 1936: Mr. & Mrs. Wm. R. Gardner and daughter Francis, Mr. & Mrs. John F. Balderson and sons Irvin and George, Richard Gardner and James Clark were Sunday guests at the home of Mr. and Mrs. Wm. L. Gardner. (Don't know who Wm. L. Gardner is.)

From *Denton Journal* 9 June 1950: Wm. R. Gardner, 72 years old, a well know Greensboro farmer, died Wednesday of last week at his home near town following a short illness. Services were held at Rawlings Funeral Home at 2 p.m. In charge of the services was Rev W. Lawson Jump of Denton. Burial was made in Holy Cross Cemetery on Greensboro-Denton highway. Mr. Gardner had been a member of the improved Order of Red Men for 25 years. He is survived by his widow, Mrs. Mary A. Gardner, and the following sons and daughters: Richard and William Gardner of Greensboro; Mrs. Sarah Breeding of Denton; Mrs. Margaret Ellwanger of Greensboro; Mrs. Katherine Fountain of Denton; Mrs. Pauline Fountain of Seaford; and Mrs. Frances Boyle of Sacramento, Calif. And 22 grandchildren. He also leaves two sisters, Mrs. Minnie Adams of Easton, and Mrs. Etta Raughley of Denton.

My grandmother Mary (Kibler) Gardner: She was born 10 Nov. 1886 and died 10 Aug 1972. Mary's home in 1900 was Greensboro, Maryland. The 1910 census states Mary was born in Ohio. Mary's father, Lewis Kibler, was born in 1844 in Alsac-Lorriane, Ingen, Germany. Mary's mother was Lena Kibler and was born in 1840 in Alsac-Lorriane, Ingen, Germany.

From *Denton Journal* 18 Jan 1919: Philip Kibler, age 33, died at his home near Greensboro on Tuesday. The funeral was held yesterday morning at the Catholic Church in Denton, Maryland. Interment took place in the churchyard. Surviving with the deceased mother are two brothers: Michael and John Kibler; three sisters: Mrs. August Brogley, Mrs. Wm. Gardner, and Mrs. John Newlin; also two half brothers, George L and Lena N Kibler.

From the *Denton Journal* 18 January 1930: Mrs. Magdalena

Kibler, age 82, died on Monday, Jan 13th from an illness of about two years. She was staying with her daughter, Mrs. Wm. Gardner at the time of her death. The funeral was held Wednesday morning at St. Elizabeth's Catholic church in Denton. The burial was in the cemetery adjoining the church. Kibler is survived by two sons, M.F. & John L. Kibler. Also by three daughters: Mrs. August Brogley, Mrs. Wm. Gardner, and Mrs. John Newlin; and two stepsons: I.N. Kibler and Geo. J. Kibler.

From *Denton Journal* February 8, 1936: Lewis N. Kibler, age 61 years, well-known farmer on the Greensboro Denton Road, died very suddenly Wednesday morning at 5:30 am. Mr. Kibler was apparently in good health, having been in town on Tuesday. On Saturday, he told his brother George that he did not feel so well. In the bedroom, he had an electric button to turn the lights on in the chicken house. At 5 o'clock he rose and turned the lights on and went back to bed and within a short time, he died. Mr. Kibler had spent most of his life in the area, coming to this section when he was a boy. He has always been a prosperous farmer and was well known in this section. Besides his widow, he leaves three children: Mrs. Charles Vogt, near tow; Mrs. Charles Bradford of Fort Meade, Florida; one son George at home; one brother George K Kibler; two half brothers, Michael and John Kibler; three half-sisters, Mrs. Wm. Gardner, Mrs. Lena Brogley near town, and Mrs. Ann Newlen of Landenberg, Pa. Services were held at 10 a.m. this morning at the Catholic Church in Denton, Maryland. Interment will be at the Catholic Cemetery on the Denton/Greensboro road.

Census record 1900 family members: Lewis Kibler (head of household) age 55, Lena Kibler age 59, George Kibler age 26, Michael Kibler age 23, Lena Kibler age 16, Philip Kibler age 14, Mary Kibler age 13, Annie T Kibler age 12, and Johnnie Kibler age 6.

From *Denton Journal* 11 Feb 1939: Mr. & Mrs. Wm. Gardner celebrated their 31st wedding anniversary Sunday, Feb 5th. Present were Mr. Mrs. M.F. Kibler; Mr. Geo Kibler; Mr. & Mrs. August Broghley; Mr. & Mrs. Charles Vogt and children, Charles & Robert; Mr. & Mrs. Henry Wood and children: Jackie, Charles, Edward, Robert, Marie, and Arthur; L. Kibler and Mr. & Mrs. J Richard Gardner and children: Dickie, Jean & Jimmy; Mr. & Mrs. Wm. R. Gardner and children, Barbara and Billy. Many others also attended. Late-hour refreshments were served consisting of: chicken salad, cake, and coffee. They were married in 1908.

John Richard Gardner (My Father): He was born 28 June 1909 and died 30 May 1994. His wife, Dorothy Bramble, was born 26 March 1909, in Chestertown, Maryland.

In 1910 he lived in Denton, Caroline County, Maryland, and was recorded as 9/12 year of a year old.

In the spring of 1918, he graduated from Frazier school in Willow Grove, Delaware.

1920 census: My dad lived in Delaware with his father. Their home in 1920 was in Representative District 6 Kent County, Delaware. Other household members in 1920 were: Wm. R. Gardner 46, Mary A. Gardner age 33, John R. Gardner 10, William L. Gardner age 8, Sarah E. Gardner age 6, Margaret M. Gardner age 4, Catherine Gardner age 3, and Anna P. Gardner 5/12 years old.

17 Sept. 1921: John Richard Gardner confirmed in Catholic faith at Immaculate Conception in Marydel, Maryland.

23 April 1927: Dad lived in Avondale, Pennsylvania, but spent holidays with parents in Greensboro. He was 18 years old.

9 July 1927: John R. Gardner & John Stewart of Avondale,

Pa. spent Sunday and Monday with Mr. & Mrs. Wm. R. Gardner.

26 October 1929: John Richard Gardner accepted a position in Danvers, Massachusetts and left the area.

1930 census: Daddy was 20 years old and did not live at home with his father.

28 March 1931: Mr. J Richard Gardner of Danvers Mass spent the weekend with his father.

26 March 1932: J Richard and Dorothy married in Danvers, Mass.

20 August 1927: Dad & James Brogley spent Sunday at Rehoboth Beach.

27 June 1931: Dad lived in Danvers, Mass.

From *Denton Journal* 24 August 1935: Mr. and Mrs. J Richard Gardner and children, Dickie and Jeanne, were guests of Mr. and Mrs. Wm. R. Gardner and family last week, left for home in Danvers, Mass.

Mr. Clifford Bramble of Portland, Maine, spent the weekend at the home of Mr. and Mrs. Wm. R. Gardner and family.

From *Denton Journal* 26 March 1932: Miss Dorothy Bramble, daughter of Mr. and Mrs. Alfred Bramble of Danvers, Mass., and J Richard Gardner, son of Mr. and Mrs. Wm. R. Gardner of Greensboro, were married March 9, 1932 by Rev. James Canary of Danvers, Mass. Mr. Gardner and his bride accompanied by Mr. and Mrs. Wm. L. Gardner also of Danvers are spending a week, Mr. and Mrs. John Balderson, and Mr. and Mrs. Wm. R. Gardner.

From *Denton Journal*: John Richard Gardner Sr. of Greensboro died Monday, May 30, 1994, at the home of his daughter Jean in Greensboro. He was 84. Born June 28, 1909, at Burrisville, he was the son of the late William R. Gardner and Mary

A. Kibler Gardner. Mr. Gardner was a crop farmer and an independently employed carpenter. He was a member of St. Elizabeth Catholic Church in Denton, the Knights of Columbus, Regina Coeli Council of Easton, the former Red Men's Lodge of Greensboro, Caroline County Farm Bureau, and a lifetime member of the Greensboro Volunteer Fire Company. He was also a former member of a Moose Lodge in Massachusetts. His wife, Dorothy Bramble Gardner, died Aug 19, 1989. Mr. Gardner is survived by two sons, J Richard Jr. of Laurel, De. and James D. Gardner of Henderson, Md.; two daughters, Jeanne E. Warren of Greensboro, Md. And Mary G. Patten of Seaford; a sister, Margaret Ellwanger of Greensboro; 12 grandchildren, and 18 great grandchildren.

My parents, John Richard and Dorothy Gardner, had four children: John Richard Jr. 1932, Jean Elizabeth 1934, James Donald Gardner 1938, and Mary Francis 1941.

Dorothy Bramble Gardner

Born 1909 in Chestertown, died 1989 in Greensboro, Md.

Family: Mother, Nettie E. Bramble, Father Alfred Bramble, Spouse John Richard Gardner.

1910: Lived in Baltimore, Md. At age one.

1911: Lived at Fairlee farm close to Chestertown Md.

1920: Lived in Representative District 8, New Castle County, Del. at age eleven.

6 August 1926: Graduated from Beacom College in Wilmington, Delaware.

1927: Graduated from Temple Nursing School in Philadelphia.

1932 09 March, Married to John Richard Gardner

7 December 1932: Birth of son John Richard Gardner in Danvers, Massachusetts.

30 June 1934: Birth of daughter Jean Elizabeth in Danvers.

1935: Lived in Danvers.

29 July 1938: Birth of son James Donald Gardner in Greensboro, Maryland.

1940: Lived in Caroline County, Maryland.

12 February 1941: Birth of daughter Mary Francis in Greensboro.

August 1989: Died in Greensboro, Md.

*   *   *

My first memories of my mother is when I was very young and living on the farm in Greensboro. She would put me under an apple tree and then hoe the crops in the field. I know I could not have been over two years old. I want to make one important fact clear: If there is a heaven for us to go to after death, my mother is one person who will surely be there. She gave it all during her life when I knew her, and she received very little in return. She went back to work as a nurse, often working the evening shift. She was the third-floor nurse at Easton Memorial Hospital, and then worked for the Milford Memorial Hospital until she retired. She made all the mortgage payments on the farm. I'm certain they would have sold the place if not for her making the mortgage payments.

Sometimes we had very little money coming in (most of the time), but mother could always find a way to put on a great Sunday dinner. Until my brother left for the Army, we would have six people sitting at the table. Sometimes we would have only one chicken for meat and when it got to me, I usually got the backbone piece. Mother would make soup out of the chicken feet.

I remember going to school in the wintertime and we only had a wood stove for cooking and a chunk stove for heat. In the morning, the stove would have to be lit and mother would make us some hot cereal and a cup of hot chocolate. It was so comforting, drinking the drink, and having one foot up on the stove to get warm. We did not have any inside bathroom and had to go outside for a bowel movement. Sometimes it would be so cold in the upstairs bedroom that the water bottle we put inside the bed to warm our feet would have ice in it in the morning.

Mother was the community medical care person for some of the neighbors. I remember one night hearing a stone hitting the side of the house. When my father asked what the person wanted, we were told that Vode was ready to deliver another baby. Mother would get up and go across the road and back a long lane to deliver the baby. Once, after delivering the baby she noticed what she thought was blood in the bedpan a few minutes after the delivery. She asked Vode if she was bleeding and was told that she had a rub of snuff in and had to spit.

When I was born in 1938, Dr. Stonesifer in Greensboro delivered me, and he charged only $4.00. My mother did not have the money and told him she would pay when she was able. The doctor would not give her or anybody else a bill. He said that she could pay him when she was able. This doctor kept no bill or medical records on any of the people he treated. He just treated whatever the symptom was at the time. There was a story that was told over the years where a person working at a tomato cannery had his arm severed. Dr. Stonesifer was called and reattached the arm on the spot.

Later, this person was seen at Johns Hopkins hospital, and it is said that the job was as good as they could have done in the operating room. I remember my mother telling me around

1955 that she had just paid for my birth. When this doctor died in around 1970, it is said that he had over a million-dollar estate.

Much to the dissatisfaction of other family members, my mother usually referred to me as "My Jimmie". She was always on my side, and in her eyes, I could do no wrong. It was well known that I was special to her. I remember that when she was working, I would cook dinner sometimes. Also, I would do the laundry for her. This meant heating water on the wood stove and dumping it into the washing machine. If the weather was good, I would hang the clothes outside on a line. If the weather was bad, I would hang the clothes in the kitchen.

Mother never asked for much and never got much. I remember once when we went to Wilmington, Delaware, and she got a London Fog coat. She was so proud of that coat, and I think she wore it for the rest of her life. She always just wanted to live until she was 80 years. I remember shortly after my mother's 80th birthday she told me that her body was worn out, and that she was ready to go.

My closing thoughts on my mother are that she accepted life as it was dealt to her and did not complain much. She always seemed to think that she could have accomplished much more if she was not stuck on a farm with very little connection with the professional world.

She wrote a book once and submitted it for publication to Reader's Digest, but it was not accepted, and she was very disappointed.

I have one brother and two sisters. My brother John Richard was born on December 7, 1932. He has two sons, Bill and Keith. Bill, the oldest, worked in the education field his entire life. Keith worked at DuPont for several years, then built a chicken farm and tended chickens for several years. He sold the farm for enough money to retire at an early age.

Jean was born in 1934 and had 3 children: Patricia was the oldest, and was murdered by her husband, Tom, who was much older than Patricia and very controlling. Albert, who had a successful career with DuPont; and Teresa, who earned a nursing degree and has worked nearly her entire life in the nursing field.

My youngest sister, Mary Francis, was born in 1944. She had three children: Michelle, the oldest, worked in the nursing field; Susan, who managed several stores in different locations; and Buddy, the youngest, and has worked in the maintenance field his entire life.

Random Notes

Mrs. Henry Adams was in Cordova, Maryland, and married grandfather Wm. Gardner's sister Minnie.

According to the1880 census, great-grandfather Richard J. Gardner was born about 1850. His spouse was Catherine S. McClements, born about 1855. Catherine S McClements died in 1920 in Willow Grove, De. And is buried in Greensboro, Md. Cemetery.

McClements Household members in 1880 included William McClements, age 65, born in Maryland; Allinta McClements, age 60; and Robert McClements, age 20. In 1880, both Richard J. Gardner and his wife Catherine Sarah Gardner lived with her father and mother on Kent Island. They had a two-year-old son (my grandfather, Wm.) living in the house also.

They must have not had much money or been broke to be living with her parents when they were about 30 years old with a child.

Henry Adams married Minnie Gardner (Catherin's daughter) in 1916 when he was 50 years old. They had a daughter (Mary Catherine 21919-2001) that married Harrison Bateman Lomax11 from Smyrna, Delaware) Henry died in 1932.

Minnie Gardner was born in 1880 and died in 1930 at the age of 50.

In 1882, Catherine's sister Etta W. Gardner was born, and in 1891, Catherine's sister Henrietta Elizabeth was born.